C000247193

A SUSSEX GUIDE

BIRD
WATCHING
IN SUSSEX

ROB YARHAM

INTRODUCED BY
CHRIS PACKHAM

Illustrated by
CURTIS TAPPENDEN

SNAKE RIVER PRESS

SNAKE RIVER PRESS

Book No 13
Books about Sussex for the enthusiast

Published in 2009 by
SNAKE RIVER PRESS
South Downs Way, Alfriston, Sussex BN26 5XW
www.snakeriverpress.co.uk

ISBN 978-1-906022-12-9

This book was conceived, designed and produced by
SNAKE RIVER PRESS

ART DIRECTOR & PUBLISHER *Peter Bridgewater*
EDITORIAL DIRECTOR *Viv Croot*
EDITOR *Caroline Radula-Scott*
PAGE MAKEUP *Richard Constable & Chris Morris*
ILLUSTRATOR *Curtis Tappenden*
CONSULTANT *Lorraine Harrison*

This book is typeset in Perpetua & Gill Sans,
two fonts designed by Eric Gill

Printed and bound in China

DEDICATION

For my mother and father, who taught me to love wildlife,
and for Sue, who shares that love with me

CONTENTS

FOREWORD

I have lists of birds. A 'garden list', a 'county list', a 'British list' and a 'world list', which is a distillation of all the other lists. These though are just lists, totals, names, species seen.

For most birders, their 'British list' is the most important to them, especially the total, the number of all the species seen in Britain in their lifetime, and that total is often seen as a measure of that birder's competence, dedication and seriousness. It is a badge used by others to make instant judgements. So I can't tell you what my British list stands at because you would use that one figure to put me on that subjective but apparently so important scale. We are all coy about it but I wouldn't lie about the magic number – many would, and do. But the real reason I'm not telling you is because it's not important.

Whenever I visit a person's house for the first time I seek out and peruse their book, CD and DVD collection with a critical eye. My snap judgement has been a first date breaker and the start of a lifelong friendship. In a similar vein I think you can learn far more about a birder by studying his or her 'favourites' list, so I really enjoyed reading Rob Yarham's Top Twenty. It reveals lots about the author and of course about the county's bird life.

So . . .

Hobby, yes. Nightjar, yes. Wryneck, oooh yes, a beauty! Nightingale, probably, Barn Owl, maybe, Bittern, definitely, Peregrine – come on – it's a must! But where is the Turtle Dove? The Yellow Wagtail? The Bullfinch? A Stonechat at the expense of the Wheatear!? My God, that's a Jackie Collins where F. Scott Fitzgerald should be, that's *Titanic* taking up *Apocalypse Now* space; and Buzzard instead of Sparrowhawk, that's the Bay City Rollers when it should be the Clash!

See, when it comes to entertaining geeks, lists are top of the list, and I know that you are already making your own. In truth though, I'm teasing, I reckon Rob has done a great job: lots of Sussex gems, personal accounts and studded throughout with little nuggets of information too.

One last thing though, this series of books is lovely, the illustrations, the jackets, the typeface – what a joy to hold, feel, covet and read in this wretched age of the Internet. Suitable for anyone's Christmas list, I would say.

CHRIS PACKHAM

DEDICATION

The illustrations are dedicated to my sister Janita,
whose bravery is inspiring

CURTIS TAPPENDEN

INTRODUCTION

'My heart in hiding stirred for a bird,
the achieve of, the mastery of the thing!'
GERARD MANLEY HOPKINS, *THE WINDHOVER*, 1877

When I first set out to discover birds I was determined to concentrate, for a while at least, on seeing and understanding as much as I could about our own natural heritage before venturing on wildlife trips abroad. And what diverse, rich and rewarding spectacles I found throughout Britain. There are now many parts of the British Isles that I love, especially when it comes to birds and wildlife, such as the rustling reedbeds, estuaries and harsh northern coasts of Norfolk, or the soft fields and marshes of Suffolk. At least once a year I feel the call to return to Scotland to see the eagles of Mull, hear the sounds of calling divers on calm lochans, watch a splashing otter by a ferry terminal on Shetland. But if I had to choose one place to be, where I could enjoy a variety of birds in a range of habitats all through the year, and one landscape to which I had to be faithful and loyal, it would be Sussex.

Neither my wife nor I are natives of the county, but ever since we first owned a car, starting our life together in south London, we have come to Sussex. Drawn here weekend after weekend, we'd set off early and head south down the motorway, aching to get to Pagham, Rye or Amberley as soon as we could, stretching the day as long as it would last, reluctantly heading home that night, after a day on the Downs, by the sea, or walking along the brooks.

Our love of the outdoors, of wildlife and of birds has grown and has been nurtured under Sussex skies. It was perhaps only natural that we came to live here as soon as we could. It is here where we feel at home, as if we have known Sussex – and Sussex has known us – all our lives.

Birds: a biased natural history

I've wanted to write a book about bird-watching in Sussex for years, so when I was asked I jumped at the chance. But then came the process of selection, of reviewing what I wanted to say about bird-watching sights and sites in Sussex. Many of you who know Sussex birds well may take issue with my selections of top birds and places to see them in Sussex. For instance, you may wonder why on earth I've included some species and omitted others. Well, I tender this apologia for my offence in mitigation. This is a purely personal selection of my favourite birds and sites in Sussex, coloured by my own experiences and enthusiasms, and I am sorry for any omissions or inconsistencies that may result.

This had to be a short book, an introduction to bird-watching in Sussex, and an attempt to enthuse readers – particularly those who may not have done much bird-watching or who are now only just embarking on discovering the wildlife of this beautiful county. I felt it best, therefore, to focus on the species for which I have a particular fondness or special memory, and to highlight what I consider to be the most rewarding places for finding birds. As a result, this is not an exhaustive or scientific review of the state of birds in the county.

Indeed, there are other titles that will provide an excellent and much more scientific review of the status of all species, such as the annual *Sussex Bird Report* or the *Birds of Sussex* (1996, now out of print, although work has begun to replace it), both produced by the Sussex Ornithological Society (SOS). Likewise, for a comprehensive review of many of the best places to see birds in Sussex, please refer to *Best Birdwatching Sites in Sussex* by Adrian Thomas and Peter Francis.

The SOS is a friendly group of volunteers dedicated to monitoring birds throughout Sussex and is an essential source of news and information in the county. The professional organisations, the Sussex Wildlife Trust (SWT) and the Royal Society for the Protection of Birds (RSPB), undertake much of the essential conservation and educational work throughout Sussex to try to preserve the wildlife of the county for future generations to enjoy and appreciate. The success stories, and there are a few, are down to these and other organisations, as well as many dedicated staff and volunteers. Details of Sussex bird and wildlife conservation organisations are listed at the end of this book. Please support them as you explore and enjoy Sussex.

Wildlife: lessons on our doorstep

So much has been and will be said and written about the environment, about wildlife and about the threats to the world around us. Some people and organisations, bound up in their worlds of economic development, intensive food production and transport expansion appear to regard the natural world as a form of 'window dressing', a 'nice-to-have', perhaps even distant from our day-to-day lives.

For those of us who take a walk in the early morning and hear the birdsong, watch the birds visit the feeder in our garden, see a fox run in front of our car, nature is all around us in Sussex. It's in our towns, fields, rivers, ponds and reservoirs, from the hills to the coasts, and even in our industrial estates. But we've seen with the massive declines in farmland birds, for instance, that things once common and taken for granted can, with a little neglect and thoughtlessness, become really rare.

Wildlife conservation organisations record bird and wildlife sightings in detail so we can watch trends and densities in populations. Once we know what's going on we can begin to understand why it's happening. Understanding the science – the observed effects of pollution, of climate change, of intensive farming – leads to understanding the world around us. When environmentalists bang on about protecting wildlife, they're not just saving a few rare birds, a butterfly here, a water vole there, they're trying to protect the world that we're a part of and that has bred and nurtured us.

Perhaps that's why the time we spend in the wild, watching and listening to the natural world, is so soothing and healthy for us. However 'evolved' we are, obsessed with our daily lives, with making money, or watching the football, the natural world is still there, sometimes pushed to the margins but always able to heal and nurture our well-being, perhaps appealing to something primeval, buried deep in our genetic memory, that tells us that this is where we came from. We may have taken from it for thousands of years, but the natural world still gives us something precious. The least we can do is to protect and nurture it in return. And by saving the life all around us, perhaps we have a chance of saving ourselves.

How to go bird-watching

If you've only just begun to watch birds or wildlife, the prospect may appear a little daunting – all those species, all their calls and sounds. Start with those most under-used, and cheapest, pieces of bird-watching equipment – your ears. Listen to the birdsong around you. There may be one predominant song. Is it short or long, and what are its main sounds or phrases? Listen to an identification video or CD and try to pick out that song. Slowly, with experience, you'll recognise more songs and learn to associate them with each bird.

So far, so not terribly expensive. Soon, it will become apparent that seeing the birds in detail will help to identify them. And there is nothing to compare with seeing a bird close up – even common birds are startlingly beautiful when magnified – and that means you'll need some good optics. Binoculars can range from the not very cheap to the ludicrously expensive, so go to a good specialist shop (such as at the RSPB's Pulborough Brooks) and ask for their advice. A telescope and tripod will become essential for seeing small birds or birds that are far away.

So, over time, and by visiting different places – including those in this book – you'll see, hear and learn more. And before you know it, you'll be experiencing the wonders of the natural world all around you. What could be more fun and awe-inspiring than that?

Acknowledgements

I am indebted to the help of many others, directly and indirectly, in writing this book: to my understanding and supportive wife, Sue, to Peter Bridgewater, Viv Croot and Lorraine Harrison at *Snake River*, and to many county bird-watchers and authorities on bird-watching, including Nick Paul, Audrey Wende and Alan Perry of the Sussex Ornithological Society and Adrian Thomas of the Royal Society for the Protection of Birds. And lastly, of course, I am most grateful to Chris Packham for providing the foreword.

Rob Yarham, *August 2008*

PART ONE

TOP 20 SUSSEX BIRDS

There have been many occasions in the field when I've bumped into another bird-watcher and asked the time-honoured question, 'Much about, then?' only to be greeted with a grumpily muttered, 'Nothing much'. This is invariably followed by a list of rather decent birds that you'd be pleased to see in your garden or in any other circumstances when not specifically out looking for birds. I am guilty of this myself.

The aim of bird-watching is quite simply to seek pleasure in the natural world but you do not need to see a rare species every day to enjoy watching birds. Every bird can be a source of joy and education, even the starling in your garden is beautiful and fascinating to watch. Yes, some of the birds I describe here are rare and some only occasionally visit Sussex, and, yes, some can be hard to see, but all of them are special in some way and I believe all are representative of the experience of bird-watching in Sussex.

There are many more I could have included if I'd had the space, but the birds in this book are just a taste of the beauty and wonder available on your doorstep, not just from the bird world but from the wildlife of Sussex. I've also listed just a few of the best places to see each bird and more sites and their details are provided in the subsequent Favourite Sites section and on pages 88-9.

BARN OWL

TYTO ALBA

There can hardly be a better known bird of the British countryside than the barn owl. Even those with little interest in birds or wildlife know a barn owl when they see one. As the white bird floats across their path, they pause and smile, a look of recognition and wonder on their faces.

And this, I think, is indicative of a welcome sea change in attitudes to wildlife since World War II. Many accounts of the natural history of birds and other wildlife can make very depressing reading – declines in breeding populations, persecution, destroyed or neglected habitat, insensitive development or intensive agricultural practices – and yet we have come a very long way in our perception of wildlife in 60 years.

The barn owl is a demonstrable case in point. Only a few generations ago, its nocturnal habits and ghostly white colouring – together with its unearthly shrieking calls – meant that it was little understood and was even feared by many who encountered it. The barn owl was thought to be a harbinger of death and a dead barn owl was sometimes nailed to a door to ward off evil spirits. It is easy to see how so much sinister folklore became associated with it, like that other bird of the night, the nightjar (see p. 34). Without street and car lights, darkness in the countryside was, well, very dark, really. And in this blackness of the night people would encounter a spectral white shape, moving through the air, shrieking. Some barn owls have even been reported to 'glow' at night, as a result, so it is thought, of picking up luminescent fungi on their feathers from the decaying wood within tree hollows where they nest. More commonly, the barn owl nests in barns or old buildings, and so it is easy to see how frightening a luminous apparition, with a skull-like face and black empty eyes, flying around an old house would have seemed to a surprised countryman walking home after a drink or two.

Thankfully, the barn owl is no longer subject to such superstition, and it doesn't get nailed to many doors today – now a protected species, killing the bird is illegal. Thanks to education and wildlife films we live in a world that has begun to appreciate this beautiful bird for what it really is. And yet, sadly, that doesn't mean it's no longer threatened by us. They like to hunt for their favourite prey of small rodents – mainly voles – on the grass verges beside our busy roads as well as in the safety of fields. In 2006 alone, 13 barn owls were found dead as a result of car impacts on Sussex roads. There were probably many more unrecorded. In addition, the growth in barn conversions and the demolition or redevelopment of old buildings in the last 20 years have meant that many owls have been evicted from nesting sites. As a result, around 80 breeding pairs were recorded in Sussex in 2006, as opposed to an estimated 100 to 150 pairs in the 1970s.

But help is at hand. There is a number of dedicated volunteers who have made it their particular mission to help these wonderful birds by putting up nest boxes on buildings in likely areas. And it seems to be working. The decline has been stopped, although numbers do fluctuate according to the amount of voles and the weather – the colder and wetter it is during the breeding season, the fewer voles they will find to feed their owlets.

And while that may not seem a huge conservation success, it does demonstrate a great change in society's attitudes to the bird and that, for me, shows that there's hope for all wildlife, not just the barn owl.

Top Sites

◉ *Waltham Brooks* all year (see p.82)   National grid ref. TQ0316
◉ *Amberley Wild Brooks* all year (see p.56)   National grid ref. TQ0314
◉ *Pulborough Brooks* all year (see p.74)   National grid ref. TQ0516

BITTERN

BOTAURUS STELLARIS

The bittern is a secretive and elusive bird, which for me undeniably adds to its magic. Skulking in the reedbeds, it is famous for its deep 'booming' call – often characterised as someone blowing across the top of a bottle. The boom, or more accurately the '*ha-boom*' if you hear them close to, is made by the male as a way of advertising his presence, both to warn other males off his territory and, Barry White-like, to entice the 'ladeez'. If male bitterns encounter each other, however, they reveal a more macho side to themselves – they often engage in combat, sometimes to the death.

The bittern has become one of the 'totem' species of bird conservation in Britain. This is mainly thanks to the efforts of the RSPB – and other wildlife conservation groups, such as the Norfolk Wildlife Trust – who, with European and British government support, have spent much time studying these birds and creating new habitats to encourage them to expand in numbers. Nationwide, the bittern has seen some growth in breeding success mainly in its East Anglian reedbed heartland. In 2008, 75 male birds were heard calling in 33 sites around the country, up from the 11 recorded calling only ten years previously.

Sadly, there are no records of the bittern breeding in Sussex. A fairly challenging bird to see even in its breeding grounds, it is a scarce winter visitor to the county and there are no records of it booming. Only 15 birds were seen – all but one during the winter months – during 2006.

The very elusiveness and rarity of a bird undoubtedly adds to its charisma. I remember the thrill of seeing one for the first time, after many attempts, one summer's evening at Minsmere in Suffolk. The sun was dipping towards the horizon, casting a yellow glow across the shimmering reed heads, from where I could hear the rhythmic chatter of the reed warblers. It first appeared at the edge of the reeds, standing in what is known as 'the bittern stance', upright with its long sharp beak pointing to the sky and its large bright eyes staring out at me through the reeds. The bittern used its streaky camouflage to blend with the surrounding reeds before slowly emerging into the open. As it crept, carefully and deliberately from one pool to another, looking for fish and amphibians, it placed its huge feet one in front of the other. The light picked out its golden and dark brown markings, its honey-coloured feathers shimmering with the oil it uses to waterproof itself.

It is a sight I've never forgotten and never tired of seeing again, as I have many times, but always in East Anglia – that is until a few years ago. It was a cold winter's evening at Burton Mill Pond, near Petworth, when I watched a similar performance at the edge of the reeds. Being able to see one of my favourite birds just a few minutes from home is one of the reasons I feel blessed to live in Sussex. These days, one or sometimes two bitterns are seen at Burton Mill most winters, either lurking at the edge of the reeds, or flying across the water.

Burton Mill is one of the two major sites in Sussex for seeing bitterns, the other being Castle Water at Rye Harbour – although they can pop up almost anywhere where there are reeds and water. Sightings at Rye, from the viewing platform at the north end of Castle Water, are regular and relatively reliable, as sometimes several bitterns fly in to roost towards dusk on a winter's evening. A bittern in flight recalls a large owl, with its broad brown wings beating languidly.

Top Sites

◎ *Rye Harbour Local Nature Reserve,*
  Castle Water, regular in winter (see p.77)   National grid ref. TQ9418
◎ *Burton Mill Pond, near Petworth, occasional in winter (see p.65)*   National grid ref. TQ9718

COMMON BUZZARD

BUTEO BUTEO

In northern England or Scotland, they call it the 'tourist's eagle', in a slightly disparaging sense – disparaging, that is, to both the buzzard and the tourist. The common buzzard is often regarded with a certain amount of snobbery as not being quite the 'real thing' – the golden eagle – and at a great distance it can sometimes be hard to tell the difference between the two birds. Smaller and more animated in flight than the golden eagle, it propels itself with a flap-flap-glide when it isn't soaring. The buzzard also has a much shorter, broader tail and broader, shorter wings than the eagle; the shallow 'v' profile of the wings also differing. Not that you'll see too many golden eagles in Sussex.

Until recently, you wouldn't have seen too many buzzards in Sussex either. Driven to breeding extinction in the county by 1882, with a small breeding population re-established in the 1950s, numbers of buzzards were probably kept down by persecution (as still happens in northern England and in Scotland), by the effects of farming chemicals on the ecosystem (as with the peregrine falcon), and by the unpleasant bout of myxomatosis that decimated the rabbit population, an important food source for buzzards. But today, with all those negative factors more or less eliminated in the south-east of England, this large hawk seems to be making a comeback, including in Sussex.

The county held between just one and seven pairs from 1965 to 1976, but although there was a reintroduction programme in the

Ashdown Forest in the 1970s, today's 250 breeding pairs are thought to be mostly the result of the natural influx of buzzards from outside Sussex.

The best time for seeing a buzzard is usually around the middle of the day, when there is enough pressure and a little cloud cover to generate thermals, the upward draughts of warm air that help to keep them airborne. A buzzard will expend the least effort it can and will often sit for hours in a tree or on a post – and wait for the right conditions. Taking off requires laborious flaps to lift its large frame into the air, but once safely seated in a thermal, the buzzard's soaring glide seems effortless and majestic. It is not uncommon to see four or more birds in the air together – even eight in West Sussex in autumn – with their broad wings and finger-like wingtips outstretched, circling and spiralling into the sky. Every time I see these noble birds my heart soars with them.

You can see buzzards in almost any part of Sussex now, particularly during the spring or autumn migration when the county's population is joined by travelling birds. But the best places to look for buzzards are over large clumps of woodland – their roosting or nesting sites – or over nearby hills, as they use the upwards gusts of air being deflected off the ground to gain height. You may even see one sitting on a post by the roadside, watching for rodents. The brown colouring of buzzards can be extremely variable, ranging from very pale, and even rarely predominantly white, to the much darker brown birds. All adult birds display a pale 'U' shape across their breasts, however, with dark or black trailing edges on the underside of their wings, and a black 'terminal band', a bar, at the end of their tails.

Occasionally you may hear the buzzard's call or 'mew', a *'peeyay'* sound that carries out across the trees and landscape. It is a sound evocative of a spring day in the British countryside and, fortunately for us, it is now much easier than it used to be to hear the buzzard's cry over the Downs of Sussex.

Top Sites

DARTFORD WARBLER

SYLVIA UNDATA

Once known by its old country name of 'furze wren', the insectiverous Dartford warbler is a handsome little bird, and a real favourite among Sussex birders. Mostly seen on its favoured and rare habitat of heather-populated heathland, the Dartford warbler is distinctive and distinguished, the males displaying rich, wine-red throat and underparts, grey cap and back, and piercing red eye.

A relatively secretive and therefore charismatic bird, the 'Darty' quite often first reveals its presence with its scratchy song – mutterings from deep within the dense undergrowth. Then you might catch a sight of a dark, long-tailed silhouette scooting across the heather and diving behind a gorse bush, the favoured source of food including spiders and caterpillars. If you're lucky, though, a bird might suddenly emerge out into the open and sing from the top of a bush, or even a tree, to find love or, more likely, declare its territory. Seemingly top heavy, with a large head and stocky little body, the warbler's long, expressive tail will flick up and down to counterbalance its jerky movements. The sight of a Dartford warbler always guarantees me a warm feeling of satisfaction and joy, even if I have seen little else all day. This may be partially down to the bird's rarity in the UK, with southern England being on the northernmost edge of its European breeding range.

The Dartford warbler's status in Britain has fluctuated since it was first discovered in 1773; two birds were shot on Bexley Heath near

Dartford in Kent and the species was subsequently named after the unfortunate pair. It was, in fact, believed that demand for the birds' skins, eggs and nests among collectors during the subsequent 150 years led to its virtual extinction in Britain. However, modern research shows that, more recently, the two most significant factors in the bird's decline were the loss of its heathland habitat and cold winters.

The records of breeding in Sussex seem to bear this out. A combination of hard winters and agricultural expansion into the bird's traditional strongholds on the slopes of the eastern South Downs during and just after World War II resulted in no birds being recorded in the county at all between 1947 and 1960. Numbers then rose and fell to between one and 23 pairs from 1960 to the 1990s. Since then, numbers have undergone a real resurgence, and birds regularly breed on certain heathlands in the county. This has led to the Dartford's current county status as being a 'fairly common but localised resident' ('fairly common' meaning between 101 and 1,000 pairs), with the most recent survey undertaken during 2006 recording a maximum number of 101 breeding territories in Sussex. The proximity of breeding sites on Surrey and Hampshire commons and the bird's ability to raise up to three broods in a successful year mean that, in combination with a series of mild winters, their numbers can increase further, but there is no room for complacency. It only takes a few cold winters, scrubbing over, and increased use of heathland for recreation, to wipe out any gains.

Much has been made in the local and national news media of the little bird being used by conservationists to halt the tide of housing development. This is an exaggeration of the position of bodies such as the RSPB, which has expressed legitimate concerns about the sprawl of housing development resulting in the isolation of heathland habitats and increased recreation, including dog walking, that can severely affect the breeding success of several heathland species.

Top Sites

GREY PARTRIDGE

PERDIX PERDIX

I once asked my father, somewhat naively, what he thought his favourite bird was. He sat in silence for a few moments and then said, 'I suppose my favourite bird is the one I'm looking at.' The more I see, the more I find that even a common bird in the garden can surprise me with its beauty – and yes, that even includes the wood pigeon – or unusual behaviour. Whenever I profess a love of a particular bird, my wife simply replies, 'But you love them all.' However, if pushed, I would have to say that the grey partridge has to be one of my all-time favourite birds.

On the face of it, the grey partridge is not a spectacular bird, and it may be considered by some to be a little drab or even pedestrian, especially when compared to the immigrant red-legged – or French – partridge. The red-legged partridge is a bit of a dandy of a bird, with a distinctive white and black face, bright red bill and eye ring, and white and black streaked bib and flanks. The grey partridge, on the other hand, is less showy and is harder to see than the extravagant 'foreigner'.

But when you are lucky enough to see one properly and close, it is a revelation. I remember seeing my first grey partridges from West Mead hide on Pulborough Brooks RSPB reserve many years ago. It was early morning and, huddled together in the long grass, a group – or covey – of six birds sat together, anxiously looking about. As I watched, the sun broke through the clouds and seemed to pick the partridges out for special attention. The light caught their pale orange faces and grey bills and shone on their mottled grey feathers and the reddish-brown barring down their sides. You could just about make out the male's dark brown belly patch among the undergrowth. As if in reply to the sunshine, the male started to make the distinctive '*kierrrek*' call, repeating it several times. It was a sound that was once common throughout the countryside. After a while, they slunk off through the grass and out of view.

I haven't seen grey partridges at Pulborough for quite a while. Reserves, although fulfilling an essential purpose of providing carefully managed habitat for a range of wildlife, can only do so much when a large part of the surrounding countryside is not managed for wildlife. With the recent passing of set-aside – the government-sponsored scheme to encourage farmers and landowners to preserve some areas for wildlife – and with economic pressure to grow more intensive crops of cereals for biofuels, I fear that things could get worse for some species.

In fact, new farming pressures could spell disaster for the humble and once-abundant grey partridge. The total estimated population in Britain has crashed from the one million or so pairs in the 1950s to around 70,000 pairs today. Grey partridges are fairly sedentary and therefore vulnerable to loss of habitat, with small groups becoming isolated from each other and less likely to find new breeding partners.

Today, it seems, grey partridges are being pushed to a few pockets on the Downs and the county's coastal margins, with Pagham, Selsey, Barnham, Climping and Rye Harbour being reliable spots to see them.

Whether it is the grey partridge's natural nervousness, its open, 'honest' features, its understated elegance, or whether it is simply the fact that it needs our help that makes me so fond of them, I'm not really sure. But I do know that I'll continue to have a special place in my heart for this special bird.

Top Sites

◗ *Climping* all year (see p.88)   National grid ref. TQ0000

◗ *Sandhill Marsh*, West Wittering,
   near East Head National Trust, all year (see p.85)   National grid ref. SZ7798

◗ *Pagham Harbour* occasional, all year (see p.69)   National grid ref. SZ8596

HEN HARRIER

CIRCUS CYANEUS

For many who love wildlife, the sight of a hen harrier, gently pushing through the air, with an elegant flap-flap of its wings, constantly looking, looking for prey in the grass below, is a special experience. Whether the bird is a brown female, a young bird (both known as 'ringtails' because of the white band on their rump) or a male with its feathers the purest and palest of greys – almost white in the sun – and black wing tips, we are lucky to see as many as we do in Sussex. The majestic lightness of the bird's flight and the rarity of the view – as a result of the usual suspects, habitat loss and persecution – make it a romantic image of beauty surviving in adversity. The hen harrier is truly an iconic bird.

Being such a totem of conservation also makes the bird a flashpoint for argument between conservationists and gamekeepers. There have been well publicised cases of hen harriers being poisoned or shot, and nests, eggs and even chicks destroyed, all guaranteed to anger birders who value these stunning birds. On the other side of the argument are those – mainly gamekeepers and a few championing songbirds – who believe that the unfettered expansion of harriers and birds of prey generally will reduce populations of other birds, such as songbirds, waders and grouse. Such people ignore the fact that a predator is not inclined to eat its prey to extinction and indeed the overall ratio of predator to prey tends to remain the same no matter what the numbers of prey, unless affected by human intervention. They also ignore the fact that most of the 500 or so pairs are to be found only in the remote parts of north and west Scotland, the Scottish isles, northern Wales and western Ireland. There were only two known nests in England in 2008, and a suspicion remains that a number of moors in northern England and the Scottish borders that ought to provide a home for hen harriers are kept free of them by keepers and landowners concerned for the success of their grouse populations.

But all this distracts from the beauty of a hen harrier, a beauty that it is our privilege to see as the birds pass through in spring and autumn, or stop over through the winter. As many as about a dozen birds over-winter in Sussex – including at Rye Bay, Ashdown Forest and the Arun Valley – and it is these birds that you are most likely to see from November to January quartering grassland, marsh or reedbed for voles, their favoured prey. The harrier's circular face resembles an owl's 'facial disc' and acts as a sophisticated listening device which gathers all available sound from the ground below and channels it into the bird's ears. A vole rustling through the grass will catch the harrier's attention and it will turn and dive, talons-first into the undergrowth.

I have often watched a hen harrier float over a riverside marsh towards dusk, sometimes at close quarters, its attention fixed on searching for food. Occasionally, the bird will look up, its eyes drilling into me, and for one small moment I experience a connection with a truly wild creature and the world around me, all thoughts of my own petty existence gone. It is only when the bird moves away again, out of view, that I feel the harsh winter cold bite into my flesh and bring me out of my trance.

Once spring has passed, they are gone – back to their breeding grounds on northern moorland by April. Every autumn, I rush down to my favourite spots to look for them, waiting for their return...

Top Sites

- *Amberley Wild Brooks* winter (see p.56) — National grid ref. TQ0314
- *Waltham Brooks* winter (see p.82) — National grid ref. TQ0316
- *Rye Harbour Nature Reserve, Castle Water, winter (see p.77)* — National grid ref. TQ9218

HOBBY

FALCO SUBBUTEO

First, the important question: does 'subbuteo' have anything to do with football, particularly that table-top game that was all the rage 30 years ago? In a way, yes it does. The game's Tunbridge Wells-based inventor, Peter Adolph, wanted to call his creation 'the hobby' but was unable to register that name, so he settled on the Latin name for the hobby falcon (which means 'smaller than a buzzard' – not the most helpful aid to identification).

Similar to a peregrine in colouring, but slightly blacker, with more clearly delineated facial markings and 'red britches' at the tops of the legs in adult birds, the hobby is a more slender, elegant and aerobatic bird. Prim and proper when perched, the hobby is brazenly flamboyant in the air. It puts its flying skills to good use by hunting for insects, particularly dragonflies, and small birds, such as martins and swifts on the wing. In fact, with its turn of speed and pointed, swept-back wings, the hobby does look rather like a large swift – convergent evolution in the two species obviously adapting to the needs of aerodynamics.

Hobbies return to our air space from their African wintering grounds in the spring, and they are seen arriving at coastal sites from mid-April onwards. Many birds move north to their breeding grounds elsewhere, but some do stay to breed. Records of hobbies breeding in Sussex are notoriously thin, but then it is pretty difficult to track down their nesting sites. Going by display behaviour and numbers in the summer, it is believed that there were at least four territories in 2006, but this is thought to be grossly under-representing their status and that there are many more, particularly in the west, where the bird can regularly be seen over heathland. Previous years' records indicate that as many as 40 to 50 pairs may breed in the county, but we don't really know. They head off south once more in late September and early October.

Where are the best places to see them? Now that's a tricky one. They do move around a lot and, as stated above, their breeding sites are hard to pin down, but they are most often seen on spring and summer evenings hawking for their favoured prey of dragonflies over Sussex heathland, particularly where the ground is damp or where there are ponds and pools to attract their food. But they can turn up anywhere.

One late April afternoon my wife and I set off to look for hobbies at a likely spot, where we were rained on with a disappointing ferocity. Disconsolate, we had returned home, only for the skies to clear over our house and patches of blue to mock us. Determined, or simply obstinate, if you like, we decided instead to take a walk nearby, along a short stretch of the River Arun near our home. After an engaging hour, watching vivid yellowhammers calling – iridescent in the clear evening light – and scratching whitethroats, we were happy with what we had seen.

And then the hobby appeared, diving down towards the river, dodging the waterside trees. It was unmistakeable. The elegant charcoal pointed primaries flicked to gain speed at ankle-scything height. The purposeful, skilful, darting flight low over the water. The snatch of the feet at a dragonfly, invisible from where I was standing. The streaking on the breast, the red-britched leg coverts. It snatched again, transferring its catch from its talons to its beak in mid-air. It rose up from the river, to turn and attack its food run over the water's surface again.

It was a dazzling, 'showboating' display of masterful wing- and footwork, like the footballer Cristiano Ronaldo at his best.

Top Sites

❯ **Pulborough Brooks** *spring & summer (see p.74)*　　　　National grid ref. TQ0516

❯ **Ashdown Forest,** *anywhere over heathland, spring & summer (see p.62)*

❯ **Amberley Wild Brooks** *spring & summer (see p.56)*　　　National grid ref. TQ0314

LAPWING

VANELLUS VANELLUS

Some readers may be wondering at my omission of waders so far – those mostly dull-looking birds that inhabit our watery grasslands, marshes, coasts and estuaries and wander about in the mud using their long beaks to drill down for energy- and nutrient-rich worms, molluscs and crustaceans. Well, if I had to choose a favourite wader of Sussex, I'd be inclined to pick the lapwing.

The lapwing is the largest – at around 12 inches (30 cm) long with a 28-inch (70-cm) wingspan – and most common of the group of waders known as plovers, and has been a familiar bird of British farmland and upland grassland for hundreds of years. It is a bird that I associate with my first bird-watching trips to Sussex, as it seemed to be the key species at my favoured haunts, Pulborough Brooks and Pagham Harbour. It is also special to me because it was the very first wader I managed to positively identify when I was a boy. That this was not a particularly blinding piece of complex species identification matters to me not one jot.

At a distance, lapwing appear as black and white birds, with a buoyant, flappy flight. Although widespread, they only occur in small groups in Sussex during the breeding season, which swell to large flocks in the winter when they are joined by continental birds. Soaring and tumbling into the air with a loud, rising '*peee-whip*' call (the origin of their common name of 'peewit') at the least provocation, or in breeding display, they are obvious and characteristic birds of grassland.

See one more closely and their markings, which appear merely distinctive from a distance, suddenly become breathtaking. The black feathers on the bird's wings and back shimmer a dark, oily green, bluish in some light, with a small mauve patch by its shoulder. This contrasts with the stark white underparts and rump, black and white face and jet black breast. A remarkable, long, rakishly swept, black tuft flicks up from the back of the bird's head. Such plumage would render it a star if it were a rare bird of the Amazon, but our long-term familiarity with the lapwing seems to have bred a certain disregard for it, if not contempt. The threats to the lapwing seem to generate less interest among the media and public than those to that other farmland bird, the skylark (*see p.42*), which has more of an iconic status in our culture.

Rather than being celebrated, the lapwing has been sneered at. Chaucer's *Parliament of Fowls* characterised it as 'the false lapwynge, ful of trecherye' and even the collective noun for lapwing is a 'deceit'. And all the noble little bird has ever done to deserve this reputation is to distract predators from its nest, a shallow, lined scrape in the ground, by feigning injury with an outstretched wing.

On the other hand, the lapwing was once appreciated for its eggs and meat, both being harvested in large quantities during the 19th and early 20th centuries. This resulted in substantial declines in breeding lapwing by the first half of the 1900s, after which it began to recover slightly. And then the effects of modern farming practices kicked in and numbers of lapwing went into decline again. The national population has fallen more than 50 per cent in the last 20 years.

The records of the Sussex Ornithological Society show that lapwing have preferred mixed farmland in the county, nesting among spring-sown cereal crops and feeding on adjacent grass fields, and as this habitat has changed so their numbers have decreased – around 70 pairs were confirmed to have bred in Sussex in 2006.

Top Sites

⊚ *Pulborough Brooks* all year (see p.74) National grid ref. TQ0516
⊚ *Pagham Harbour* all year (see p.69) National grid ref. SZ8596
⊚ *Pevensey Levels*, Horse Eye Level, all year (see p.89) National grid ref. TQ6208

LITTLE TERN

STERN ALBIFRONS

As a wildlife conservationist, you have to get used to severe ups and downs in life – a sort of wildlife news-generated bipolar disorder. There are the highs of victory – learning of increases in a particular species or the purchase of a new reserve, for instance – and then there are the lows of hearing that other battles may have been lost.

As things stand as I write this, the little tern seems to be just clinging on as a breeding bird in Sussex. This sweet sea bird – looking rather like a little white swallow with a bouncing, jerky flight – is usually the last of the terns to return to its breeding sites on open sand or shingle beaches along the coast in early April. But its preference for these nesting sites is proving to be its undoing, and now the little tern's plight is as delicate as the bird itself seems to be.

In 1983-84, a survey of breeding sea birds reported a total of 93 pairs nesting in wardened reserves at Chichester, Pagham Harbour and Rye Harbour. In 2006, 24 pairs were recorded nesting at Rye Harbour (including three pairs on Flat Beach) and three pairs were recorded at Ella Nore in Chichester Harbour. Nine chicks fledged that year at Rye, but four others disappeared as a result of predation. Since then, no young were raised at Rye in 2007 and the birds left early, and not one nested there in 2008. On the positive side, little terns have returned to breed at Pagham Harbour in both 2007 and 2008. So it is hoped that they will continue to breed there successfully in the future.

What is known is that the twin perils of predation (by foxes, kestrels, little owls and others) and disturbance by humans have affected the breeding success of little terns severely. Unfortunately for little terns, people also like to be beside the seaside as much as they do, especially during the height of the summer and holiday season which of course coincides with the height of the breeding season. The gradual encroachment on beaches by building since World War II, as well as the high number of people enjoying leisure activities and walking dogs on them have all conspired to make life pretty tough for these nervous birds. Other forms of protection provided by conservationists, such as fencing off areas of beach to keep predators and people at bay or providing small covers to keep predators off their nests, do not seem to have helped. Even high tides coinciding with rough seas have been known to wash their nests away.

At only 9½ inches (25 cm) long with an 18-inch (45-cm) wingspan, the little tern appears about half the size of the common tern, and is roughly the same size as a starling. In summer it has a black cap, a white forehead and distinctive black eye stripes which give it the appearance of a diminutive masked super hero. In summer, its delicate beak is yellow with a black tip. When fishing, it hovers low over the water with rapid beats of its slender, elegant wings, and it dives to catch fish again and again, much more frequently than the larger terns.

Terns can also be seen on passage from coastal sites in the county, mostly in the spring as well as at the end of the summer, with a few hundred being reported flying past every year. But it would be a sad loss if all we ever see of this delicate, flitting sea bird are the occasional spring and autumn migration fly-pasts at the traditional sea-watching sites. Let's hope that this chapter is more of a celebration than an epitaph for the little tern in Sussex and that they do come back from the brink and breed in larger numbers again. After all, one good tern deserves another.

Top Sites

❯ *Pagham Harbour* spring & summer (see p.69)   National grid ref. SZ8596

❯ *Rye Harbour Nature Reserve,* beach, spring & summer (see p.77)   National grid ref. TQ9317

❯ *Thorney Island* spring & summer (see p.80)   National grid ref. SU7602

NIGHTINGALE

LUSCINIA MEGARHYNCHOS

I may be right, and I may be wrong, but I'm perfectly willing to swear, that every time I go to my civic amenity site, a nightingale sings in the bushes there. Vera Lynn was almost certainly wrong about the nightingale in Berkeley Square – it was probably a robin singing through the night – but all you really need to do if you want to hear a true master of birdsong at work, is visit a number of key sites in Sussex, including my local rubbish tip in Billingshurst.

Once you have heard a nightingale, you couldn't possibly mistake it for a robin, wren, blackbird – or for anything else. The liquid, trilling, melodic perfection of a nightingale's song has been much eulogised, particularly by the Romantic poets, who so often looked to nature for inspiration. However, nothing can prepare you for the control, dynamism, range or almost unnatural-sounding noises that the little bird emits. One study found that a nightingale can use nearly 250 different phrases composed from 600 basic sounds. Each song is compiled differently, sometimes starting with a deafening trill or a long, quiet note, building up in a massive crescendo to a sudden suspenseful silence, passing from one phrase to another with a maestro's nuance and flair. The nightingale is a soloist of extraordinary perfectionism.

And, as befits all such maestros, the nightingale is also extraordinarily difficult to work with. Seeing one is not at all easy, and some would say a little disappointing. The bird is a typical 'LBJ', or little brown job, to use a favourite old birder's phrase. The shape of a small, plain thrush, a little larger than a robin, the nightingale has brown upper parts and light brown underparts, and a pale eye ring, although you may get a flash of its chestnut reddish-brown tail and rump, if you're lucky.

Your best chance of seeing a nightingale is in the first few days after they return each year to their traditional breeding sites around the middle of April. However, it is possible to spot them at coastal sites as they first come in a little before then. The new arrivals happily broadcast their wares and freshly acquired territory from relatively prominent branches in these early days. As April turns into May, though, they soon disappear into the undergrowth.

As is often the case with skulking birds, seeing a nightingale is not so much about range as it is about angle. It is best to avoid actually climbing into the thicket with the nightingale to try to see it. Naturally, such harrassment will always result in the bird disappearing into a further, denser thicket. It is much better to stand well back and, using the focus wheel on your binoculars, carefully zoom in on the spot where you can hear it, looking from different angles, to try to see past the branches and foliage. Patience may, sometimes, be rewarded. And if it isn't, it doesn't really matter because the vocal performance alone is worth the price of admission anyway.

The nightingale has declined in its strongholds across southern Britain and the Sussex population seems to have experienced similar drops, although sightings seem to have been holding steady in the county for the past few years. The nightingale tends to favour dense thickets and undergrowth which are thought to be disappearing with the widespread loss of ancient woodland and overgrazing by burgeoning deer populations. The most reliable sites to hear, or even to see, a nightingale are Pulborough Brooks and Ebernoe Common. And, of course, Billingshurst's civic amenity site.

Top Sites

🔵 *Pulborough Brooks* spring (see p.74)	National grid ref. TQ0516
🔵 *Ebernoe Common* spring	National grid ref. SU9727
🔵 *Woods Mill*, near Henfield, spring	National grid ref. TQ2113

NIGHTJAR

Creeping about the countryside, far from civilisation and in the dead of night, may not be everyone's idea of fun, and it sounds like the sort of thing that might well get you locked up, but of all the spectacles available to the Sussex birder the summer night performances of nightjars are not to be missed. Once you've heard the eerie churring of these intriguing birds, you'll be hooked.

Yes, you've guessed it, the nightjar is almost exclusively nocturnal and is therefore not an easy bird to see and, as we know, that makes it all the more charismatic – a recurring theme amongst favourite birds, I find. A peculiar mix of owl and hawk (night-hawk or fern-owl are common names for the bird) the nightjar uses enhanced night vision from its large, black eyes to navigate around the landscape in the dark. The bird's wide, gaping mouth, fringed with fine 'whiskers', helps it catch night-flying insects such as moths on the wing.

Nightjars arrive from their African wintering grounds to take up summer residence on our heaths about the middle of May. Nesting on the ground – radio-tracking has recently shown that they mostly roost high in pine trees – they use their grey and brown camouflage to good effect during the daytime to hide from view.

The churring call of the male bird is a magnificently bizarre noise – a low, undulating trill that echoes across the heathland, sometimes for hours on end. Perhaps we are too familiar today with electronic sounds and special effects to be as awe-struck or even terrified by the other-worldliness of a nightjar's churring as our ancestors may have been. In southern Britain, country folk incorrectly believed the nightjar was the cause of a fatal disease in calves called 'puckeridge', which was another one of its folk names.

Nightjars declined dramatically after World War II because of the loss of their habitat and intensive farming. In 1946 there were thought to have been between 1,000 and 2,000 occupied territories in Sussex alone. Compare that post-war figure to the national survey of nightjar populations in 1992 which indicated a total of 3,000 churring birds nationwide. But, thanks to conservation work, recent years have seen a halt in the decline and even a slight resurgence in their numbers. Records of churring males in 2006 indicated around 105 territories across Sussex, on the West Sussex heathland commons and in Ashdown Forest.

To hear and see them, it is best to choose a warm, still and clear night in late May to June, and to arrive well before dusk, braving the midges, and quietly wait. Not long before dusk you'll hear the churring begin to fade in and out and gradually crescendo in intensity. Finally, if you're lucky you may see one fly, or even call from the branch of a nearby tree. Listen out for the 'kru-ik' calls and the clap of a male bird's wings above its back during a display flight. As well as creating the clap sound, this movement also shows off the bird's white wing-tip patches, and they will fly around investigating each other's performances.

To attract nightjars, I have resorted to waving my arms up and down, a white handkerchief in each hand in a sort of self-consciously demented morris dance attempting to mimic the nightjar's wing tip flashing display. I don't do this any more as many conservationists believe this disturbs the birds. Besides, anyone else present did tend to think I was a bit of a prat. And, once they'd finished their inspection, so did the nightjars, probably.

Top Sites

◉ *Ambersham Common* summer (see p.58)   National grid ref. SU9119
◉ *Ashdown Forest* summer (see p.62)
◉ *Iping & Stedham Commons* summer (see p.89)   National grid refs. SU8421 & SU8521

PEREGRINE FALCON

FALCO PEREGRINUS

Any encounter with a peregrine falcon is memorable. Its power, grace, speed and majesty are hard to match. Built for speed and to absorb the impact of a high-velocity kill, the slate grey-backed peregrine is a compact, big-shouldered shape in the sky. The bird is famous as the fastest living thing on the planet. In level flight, the bird can reach 60 mph (100 kph), but it has been estimated that it can reach a terminal velocity of up to 240 mph (380 kph).

Peregrines need their athleticism to feed on other birds, mostly caught on the wing, and are particularly partial to pigeons, although they will take birds of all sizes from goldcrests to geese. Some bird-watchers – especially males – appear to take a strange pleasure in observing kills by birds of prey. Being of an unashamedly squeamish disposition, I don't enjoy such spectacles, but the observational naturalist in me takes over. I remember watching a female peregrine being harried at a cliff nest site. Often exercised by the presence of peregrines on their cliffs, the local jackdaws made a continuous nuisance of themselves until the falcon appeared finally to tire of the attention. With breathtaking suddenness, she powered up from her perch, gaining height above the cliffs, swept back her wings, turned, rolled and dived, striking one of the offending jackdaws and killing it. Like a character in a Martin Scorsese film, the peregrine had switched from amused irritation to lethal intent in the blink of an eye. It was at once horrific and hypnotic.

Peregrines tend to live a solitary existence for most of the year until they need to breed, although pairs tend to be monogamous and will associate loosely with each other throughout the winter. The male bird is much smaller than the female, the sexual dimorphism allowing the two birds to share a territory without competition, feeding on slightly different prey. A pair will participate in bonding displays over the nest site, usually on a ledge on a cliff or tall building, in mid- to late March, just before egg-laying. Chicks hatch 29-32 days later and fledge roughly 35-42 days after that. The RSPB operates a viewing point, complete with telescopes and CCTV, at Chichester Cathedral every spring, enabling the public to observe peregrines on a nest box put in place on one of the towers by the Sussex Ornithological Society.

The peregrine was once a bird in trouble in Britain. As with many birds of prey, they were seen as a threat by gamekeepers and suffered severe persecution as a result. There was even a policy of eradication during World War II to prevent the birds catching wartime carrier pigeons on their way back from occupied France. However, it was post-war farming methods that turned out to be the main cause of reduced numbers.

Organochlorine compounds used to treat crops were identified as the culprits – significant quantities of the chemicals built up in seed-eating birds which in turn poisoned the predators feeding on these birds. In addition, the widespread use of the pesticide DDT affected birds of prey by weakening their egg shells, resulting in many nest failures. The withdrawal of DDT saw the slow recovery of some of our most spectacular birds, among them the peregrine.

Up to 12 nests were recorded along Sussex's sea cliffs in 1904 but numbers then declined to the extent that 1956 provided the last breeding record until 1990, when a pair was reported breeding at Beachy Head. Fortunately, peregrines can now be seen at several sites across the county. There were around 20 breeding pairs in Sussex in 2006.

Top Sites

◗ *Cliffs between Brighton & Newhaven* all year National grid ref. TV4499
◗ *Chichester Cathedral & city centre* spring & summer only (see p.88)
◗ *Beachy Head* all year (see p.84) National grid ref. TV5895

POMARINE SKUA

STERCORARIUS POMARINUS

A n important part of birding in a coastal county like Sussex is what I regard as that most difficult of bird-watching pursuits – sea-watching. Now, I have to admit that I do not get on very well with sea-watching. I never have, however hard I've tried. I try to get to grips with watching the dark grey, whitish shapes make their way over the grey and white waves, relying on more experienced sea-watchers present for confirmation of the birds' identities. Huddling against a sea wall to shelter from the wind, I clutch the shaking tripod in one ice-encased hand and adjust the focus with the other, squinting at the blurring morphs in the stinging sea spray, and think of all the more comfortable and less endurance-testing things I could be doing. Such as rock-climbing. Or swimming the Channel. But all this hardship is not without its benefits, one of which is spotting what is arguably the most valued of all sea birds by Sussex birders – the pomarine skua.

Known affectionately as the 'pom', it is one of the aggressive skua species, which spend much of their time at sea and are well-known for their parasitic habits – chasing other sea birds to force them to disgorge their food, which they then eat. Nice. Like the slightly larger great skuas, pomarine skuas are more inclined to be predatory of other sea birds as well, attacking them and eating them over the water. While Arctic and great skuas do nest in northern Britain – on the northernmost Scottish islands, mainly in the Orkneys and the Shetlands – pomarine skuas nest on the Arctic tundra. But they do travel past the British Isles in the spring and autumn to and from their breeding grounds, and this is when birders gather at prominent headlands along the coast to watch for them and other migrating sea birds.

Distinguishing one skua from another is a skill acquired through experience and studying the field and identification guides. The much more common Arctic skua is the bird most likely to be confused with a pom, particularly during its youth when the Arctic skua lacks its long pointed tail. Great skuas, commonly known by their Shetland name 'bonxies', are larger and stockier than poms and have a short, blunt tail.

The pom is slightly larger than an Arctic skua, however, and flies with a steadier wingbeat, similar to a gull. It also has a heavier, more barrel-chested build than the Arctic skua, but the pom's most distinctive attribute is the long, spoon-shaped tail of the adult bird. At a distance, through the spray or haze, this can just look like a long tail, but taken together with its flight characteristics it should be possible to distinguish it from the others.

As with all sea-watching, you need to catch the weather forecasts for the right conditions – strongish southerly to easterly winds which push the birds close in against the Sussex coast. Head for points such as Selsey Bill, Brighton Marina and Splash Point (at Seaford). Poms are rarely seen off the Sussex coast during the autumn. The best time to look for them is May, when they can be seen flying past on their own or in flocks, sometimes in groups as large as 20. Either way, they are impressive birds and well worth the effort.

Such is the pomarine skua's following in Sussex that there has even evolved an unofficial annual 'competition' among the keenest of Selsey's sea-watchers, with the birder seeing the most poms in a year being named 'pom king'. It's a title I'm unlikely to acquire myself, but I have the utmost respect for all those who love these spectacular birds.

Top Sites

- *Selsey Bill* April to May (see p.86) — National grid ref. SZ8592
- *Splash Point,* Seaford, April to May (see p.86) — National grid ref. TV4898
- *Brighton Marina* April to May — National grid ref. TQ3302

SHORT-EARED OWL

ASIO FLAMMEUS

The short-eared owl is another visitor from the north that can be seen in Sussex on passage in spring or autumn, or when stopping over for longer periods during the winter. It shares many of its haunts with the hen harrier, so it is not uncommon to see one where you would see the other, on flat open grassland or coastal marsh, where they hunt for voles and other small mammals.

Less showy in its flight than the hen harrier, the short-eared owl is nonetheless an equally totemic bird for me. It perfectly encapsulates the wild and lonely spirit of a bird of the north. Perhaps I am also fond of the short-eared owl because it reminds me of a favourite moor on Orkney or a young plantation on the Uists – the distant and wild Scottish island landscapes where I have seen its pale brown and white form restlessly quarter the ground.

The short-eared owl is, like the little owl, a bird that hunts by day so should be relatively easy to see. It is about the same size as a barn owl but with longer, elegant wings, and it is streaked 'dirty' yellow-cream and brown on the top of its wings, back and around its head. It can be most easily confused with the barn owl or the very similar long-eared owl, but both fly at night and roost in the day.

Perhaps it is the proportion of its wings, but I always think of the short-eared owl as a more elegant bird in flight than the barn owl. Where the barn owl floats and flutters like an oversized butterfly, the short-eared, or 'shorty' as it's known to birders, pushes itself majestically forward with light flaps of its long, stiff, board-like wings.

The short-eared owl can often be seen resting on the ground or a post and it is at these moments that you see why the bird has picked up the more traditional nickname in northern England and Scotland of 'cataface' or 'cattie face'. As with all owls – or harriers – the bird has a round facial disc, which is emphasised by the dark brown streaks that surround it and form the central ridge down its forehead. Either side of its black, sharp bill are two large, round, bright yellow eyes with black pupils. The yellowness of its eyes are enhanced by the jet black areas that surround them, as if it has overdone the mascara and eyeliner. I have often stumbled across a shorty on a winter's walk and its large eyes have always made the bird look surprised, if not exceedingly put out, by my presence. It's not mutual – finding a shorty wintering on a Sussex marsh simply makes the whole season for me.

The British population is thought to amount to about 1,000 pairs, although given their nomadic, here-one-year-not-the-next existence, their numbers do tend to fluctuate. Shorties have bred in Sussex but it is not a frequent occurrence – 10 pairs nested on Pevensey Levels in 1921 and one pair bred there in 1922. Since then, the owls have been regular autumn and winter visitors in Sussex, with up to about a dozen birds being present during some winters, but they rarely frequent the same spot year after year. For instance, the Arun Valley, including the brooks at Pulborough, Waltham and Amberley, has held one or more shorties some winters, or a bird has stayed for a few days in October or November, but none might be found there at all in other years. More reliable spots along the coast during November and December where they could be seen are Thorney Island (where they often roost), Chichester Harbour, Pagham Harbour and Rye Harbour. Birds can also be seen passing through in the spring and autumn.

Top Sites

- *Thorney Island* winter (see p.80) National grid ref. SU7602
- *Selsey West Fields* winter (see p.86) National grid ref. SZ8394
- *Amberley Wild Brooks* winter (see p.56) National grid ref. TQ0314

SKYLARK

ALAUDA ARVENSIS

To modern ears, there can be no sound more redolent of the British countryside than the happy, whistling, trilling song of the skylark. An early summer's walk across the rolling Sussex Downs or through coastal fields is made complete by the nearly constant soundtrack of the skylark's pretty, fluting notes ringing far above one's head from a tiny dot high in the bright sky.

A small bird with a tawny-brown back, slim white collar and eye-stripe, streaked upper breast and bright white underparts, the skylark also has – like the woodlark (*see p.50*) – a small crest that it raises in display or song. When disturbed it will flit short distances, displaying its white outer tail feathers and glide down to the ground.

The male skylark sings from late winter through to midsummer (it can sometimes be heard all the way through to November) and although it will sing from a post the bird is best known for its virtuoso song flights. The lark will take off from the ground and flap its way up to dizzying heights of between 300 ft (90 metres) and 450 ft (137 metres), where it will hover, its wings quivering, singing its frantic, undulating song. The song can last up to 15 minutes or so, after which it will descend and drop silently like a stone to the ground.

Universally admired though the skylark is today, the relationship between the people of Sussex and the skylark has a long, dark history. The skylark was a prized food for hundreds of years and the Sussex

Downs played the part of renowned killing fields until as recently as the 1930s. Most birds were caught during the winter when they were plump enough to eat and when numbers were swelled by over-wintering birds from the Continent. The hunters would use a net to catch them on the ground and would often work at night, using a lamp and a spinning reflector, designed to dazzle the birds before throwing a net over them. Thousands of the birds were sent to markets in Brighton, London or on the Continent and at the end of the 19th century it was recorded that 20,000-30,000 skylarks were being delivered to Leadenhall Market every day. The skylark was finally protected by law in 1931. Although the bird is still widespread with over a million breeding pairs in Britain, this is over 50 per cent fewer birds than were recorded 25 years earlier.

Again, modern farming practices appear to be the cause. The use of pesticides (which eliminates insects), converting lowland grassland to arable crops (which reduces available habitat), early silage cutting (which destroys nests) and the increased autumn sowing of cereals (which reduces the winter stubble fields that provide food for skylarks) are all thought to contribute to making life harder for the larks and for farm-land birds in general.

Estimating the current population of the skylark in Sussex is pretty difficult, although the bird is still moderately common. Numbers increase during the winter, when flocks wintering on stubble and set-aside fields are joined by more larks from the continent.

The skylark's sweet song, full of youthful, pastoral innocence and its inoffensive, shy nature make the bird so appealing to us today. In many respects the skylark represents our changing relationship with the wildlife that inhabits the countryside around us. Always admired for its song, once exploited as a food, but now recognised as threatened by our modern way of life, it is a symbol of the struggle to conserve and protect what was once commonplace but is now in decline.

Top Sites

STONECHAT

SAXICOLA TORQUATA

All right, I'll own up. You may have noticed by now that a large proportion of my feathered favourites do tend to inhabit Sussex's heaths. This is by no means unexpected, as the county has some fine lowland heaths, such as to be found at Ashdown Forest and Ambersham, Iping, Stedham and Lavington commons.

A rare and threatened habitat, lowland heathland has been disappearing fast – less than 17 per cent of Britain's heathland that was around in 1800 remains today. In 1981, it was found that only around 1,650 acres (670 hectares) of the 18,500 acres (7,500 hectares) recorded in Sussex in 1813 still existed. Like elsewhere in Britain, heaths have succumbed to pressures from development, agriculture and natural changes in the vegetation, including the expansion of areas of trees and scrub. Heathland also requires regular cutting, light grazing and controlled burning, to maintain it. Fortunately, a good deal of work is underway to restore and maintain these places.

Such pockets of remaining Sussex heathland are not just important for biodiversity, they are undeniably special places. Heaths are peaceful, quiet places, the sound deadened by the heather and sand and surrounding shelter-giving stands of trees. Although you may not see a huge number of birds, what you do see is always worth the effort, such as woodlarks (*see p.50*), Dartford warblers (*see p.20*), occasional crossbills or a hobby (*see p.26*) flitting overhead and stonechats.

Of all the heathland species, the stonechat is probably the easiest to spot. Walk across heathland in the spring or summer and you are likely to hear its alarm call first – as is often the case, the birds will see you long before you see them. Preceded by a shrill, short whistle, the '*click-clack*' sound is similar to two stones being banged together and gives the bird its name. The birds will flit and perch, clicking almost constantly, on top of prominent heather or gorse outcrops and call to each other to warn of your presence. The male birds are brightly coloured, with a distinctive jet black head, bright white collar and rusty red underparts. The female doesn't have such a black head or clearly defined collar and, in winter, a young or female bird can be mistaken for a whinchat, although a whinchat has a definitive eye stripe.

Confusion between the two species obviously did occur in the past, as the local Sussex name 'furze chat' applied equally to both birds. Even that eminent, pioneering naturalist of the 18th century, Gilbert White, may have confused the two when he determined that the whinchat stayed behind in winter – the whinchat doesn't, but many stonechats do, one of our few insect-eating birds to do so.

This tendency to stick it out in Britain during the winter does make the stonechat very susceptible to harsh winters when insects become scarce. Stonechats can raise three broods during the summer months to compensate, however, which means that their numbers can quickly recover. The dependency on insects in winter is another reason that stonechats tend to cling to the milder climate of southern Britain.

Numbers of breeding stonechats are difficult to pin down, but it is thought that there are usually around 80 breeding pairs at roughly 50 sites across Sussex, although the figure has dipped as low as the 15 breeding pairs recorded in 1986. After the breeding season, birds tend to disperse, often to coastal sites, but numbers across Sussex, including on the heaths, are increased by wintering birds from the continent.

Top Sites

- *Beachy Head* all year (see p.84)   National grid ref. TV5895
- *Ambersham Common* all year (see p.58)   National grid ref. SU9119
- *Ashdown Forest* all year (see p.62)

SWIFT

APUS APUS

Each spring, in April and May, after what seems like an eternity
since they left for Africa, I watch the sky and listen for swifts,
longing for them to return. I don't think there is another bird
sound that raises my spirits quite so much. And I am not alone in
worshipping the sweeping, scything, screaming, summer-defining swift.
For many people, no other bird represents our short, sweet summer
in quite the same way. No other bird's flight call appears to say, 'This
is the summer, seize the day,' as much as the swift's joyful, speed-freak
'*Sreeeeeeee... sreeeeeeee*'.

Swifts are truly remarkable birds – they spend almost all their lives
in the air, they feed (on flying insects), drink, mate and even sleep on
the wing and only land to nest and breed. Uniquely adapted to this aerial
lifestyle, the swift's scythe-like wing shape has evolved to reduce drag,
maximise lift and make the process of flight as energy-efficient as possible. There was a time when we believed that their physiology had been
so remarkably adapted they didn't have feet, hence their Latin name,
Apus, which means 'without feet'. Their legs and feet are actually quite
small and hunched up under their bodies, only suitable for shuffling
about in their nests. Large and black, with a little smudged patch of
white on their chins, they are often confused or grouped with swallows
and martins, with which they can often be seen feeding, but they are in
fact more closely related to the hummingbird.

Mainly associated with human habitation, swifts tend to nest in old buildings, mostly in dark cracks beneath roofs or in church towers, using small gaps in the roofs, usually in soffits or eaves, to access suitable nest cavities. But something seems to be happening to swifts in Sussex. Once-teeming urban colonies that used to number dozens of breeding birds appear to have been decreasing in size, to the extent that no colonies of more than three pairs have been reported in Sussex in recent years.

The distinguished ornithologist and environmentalist Max Nicholson once said of the swift's chosen homes, 'Paradoxically, there are in practice few nesting sites so immune from human disturbance as those under the roofs of dwellings.' Sadly, this is no longer the case. As soffits decay and are replaced, the holes and vents that swifts use to gain access to the inside of a roof are disappearing or being blocked off with wire. When the swifts arrive in spring expecting to find their usual nest and discover it's no longer accessible they will leave to find another site. Little by little, this is being repeated across the county, to the extent that our swifts are declining. With the species still plentiful elsewhere this may not seem to be too much of a problem, but the continued exclusion of swifts and a lack of alternative suitable nesting sites could change their status very quickly. It would be nice to be able to mitigate against such a disaster before it becomes too late.

Fortunately, there are solutions – it is possible to install special nest boxes, although it obviously helps if your building is near a colony, or is being 'prospected' by swifts. The Sussex Ornithological Society has launched a swift initiative and is able to provide advice. To find out more, visit *www.sos.org.uk*.

Just as suddenly as the swifts come, they are gone. By early August, the adults and fledged young alike have soared off south, heading for their African wintering grounds, and the skies are silent again, awaiting their return.

Top Sites

❯ *Lewes town centre, over West Street car park, summer*
❯ *Midhurst town centre summer*
❯ *Horsham town centre summer*

WOODCOCK

SCOLOPAX RUSTICOLA

As you will have gathered by now, I have an irritating tendency – as have many birders – to appreciate particularly birds that are rare or difficult to see, and the woodcock is certainly not the easiest bird to see, or rather to see well.

For a start, the woodcock is a bird of the night. It roosts during the daytime in dense undergrowth in woodland, and makes the best possible use of its striated, chestnut brown-coloured camouflage. In appearance it resembles the snipe, being brown and striped with a long, straight bill, but it is about a third larger with a wingspan of up to 25 inches (65 cm) as opposed to the snipe's 18 inches (46 cm). The woodcock also, it has to be said, looks a bit dumpy.

Apart from its size and habitat, the other clue to its identity are the broad bands on its crown which cross from one side to the other – the snipe's head stripes run from back to front. Its large, black, jewel-like eyes are positioned high up on its head and give it all-round monocular vision so that it can monitor the approach of possible predators as it sits, hunkered down on the woodland floor. You would be really lucky to see these distinguishing features, though. The closest many of us get is to disturb one by blundering near its roosting spot among the trees, as I did once in the woods at Ebernoe Common, near Midhurst. Stumbling into the trees from the bordering meadow, I was startled by a brown, coot-sized bird exploding into flight from the ground. It twisted up into the air and zig-zagged away from me with wings whirring, flying through the trees at about shoulder height, its drooping, pencil-like bill just visible, before dropping down out of sight.

The woodcock has always been a prime target as a game bird as it was a good source of food and had a reputation as being rather easy to catch. The bird's habit of resolutely refusing to clamber over obstacles made it pretty easy to drive them along specially created 'channels' on the woodland floor. Woodcock also prefer to fly through favourite routes between the trees, which meant that they could be caught easily by nets placed across these routes, known as 'cockshoots', and waiting until they flew into them at dawn and dusk on the way to and from their feeding spots. Their weaving flight makes them very difficult to shoot, however, which sort of evens up the odds a little.

Woodcock numbers are believed to be in steep decline now. Given their secretive habits, particularly when nesting, it is almost impossible to confirm numbers of breeding woodcock, which is why the estimate of the national breeding population is a little vague – between 5,400 and 13,700 pairs countrywide in 2000. Likewise, it would be foolhardy to make a guess at numbers in Sussex, but there were around 50 breeding territories recorded in 2006, mostly on the heathlands in the Ashdown Forest and West Sussex commons.

The best way to see woodcock is to watch at the edge of woodland, for the males' display, or 'roding', flights at dusk. Pick the right spot, and you will see the woodcock's dumpy black silhouettes circle their territory, rapidly beating their wings and making a distinctive, bizarre call – a series of frog-like, gutteral '*wuh wuh wuh-wuh*' noises followed by a high-pitched '*pssp*'.

And for those who bemoan the lack of waders in this book, the woodcock is related to the snipe and therefore counts as a wader. Sort of.

Top Sites

- *Ambersham Common* spring & summer (see p.58)
- *Ashdown Forest* spring & summer (see p.62)
- *Iping & Stedham Commons* spring & summer (see p.89)

National grid ref. SU9119

National grid refs. SU8421 & SU8521

WOODLARK

LULLULA ARBOREA

To some observers, the woodlark may appear a disappointingly brown and uninteresting little bird, a typical 'LBJ'; not a bird to go out of one's way to see, even. But I would not count myself among them. The woodlark is perhaps my favourite small bird of all.

Unlike its show-off cousin, the skylark (*see p.42*), which boasts assorted poetry and music among its many accolades, the woodlark has obviously not had such a good public relations outfit working for it. In fact, it is comparatively ignored by popular, or even highbrow, culture. Gerard Manley Hopkins, a poet with an eye – and ear – for beauty, naturally proves to be the exception to the rule, but even his poem admits that the woodlark was not as famous: 'The skylark is my cousin and he/Is known to men more than me'.

Personally, I find this lack of artistic interest baffling because if you could see the bird up close (not an easy venture, woodlarks being quite shy), you would be surprised by its handsome markings, which are more heavily delineated than a skylark's, with a reddish-brown tint to its cheek. As it flits in an undulating flight from one tree to another or to feed on the ground, you'll catch sight of its stumpy little tail and distinctive pale bar on its wings, which the skylark doesn't have.

The woodlark also chooses a less exposed and more discrete habitat than the skylark's open fields. Preferring the sandy Wealden heathlands in north-west Sussex, and some spots in Ashdown Forest, the birds seem particularly drawn to recently cleared areas of forest plantation. As the plantation matures, usually after five years or so, the woodlarks move on, feeding and breeding in another more recently cleared habitat. Although it is thought that a small proportion of Britain's woodlarks do migrate, it is a relatively sedentary species, preferring to stay fairly near to its breeding sites during the autumn and winter. Groups of wood-larks are often seen feeding on stubble in fields near their breeding areas.

It is perhaps this endearing fussiness that has proved the woodlark's downfall. The British population of woodlark crashed to an estimated 220 pairs in the 1980s with none at all recorded breeding in Sussex from 1972 until 1987. Naturally, we humans don't leave anything alone for too long, or if we do, it is not usually with wildlife in mind – until recent years, that is, when concerted efforts by the RSPB, Wildlife Trusts, National Trust and government agencies have been successful in regen-erating heathland habitat. As a result, woodlark numbers are on the rise and there are now estimated to be around 100 breeding pairs in Sussex.

There is one other trait that distinguishes the woodlark from the skylark, however, and those who know these birds will probably have been unable to resist shouting at this page: what about their song? Ah, yes – the woodlark's song. Although it is less obviously magnificent than a nightingale's – to which it has even been compared by some enthusiasts – the woodlark's mellifluous, liquid yodel is to my mind birds at their most musical. Whereas the nightingale prefers a dramatic flourish and a well-judged silence, the woodlark prefers studied, sweet trills and lilting cascades of notes; its Latin name *Lullula* is a clue to the sound. Woodlarks can be heard singing from perches on branches or the tops of trees at almost any time of year, but the best time to hear them – and see them – is on still days in February when the males begin to sing over their territory in slow, circular display flights.

Top Sites

WRYNECK

JYNX TORQUILLA

Firstly, allow me an explanatory digression: if there is one thing guaranteed to upset a bird-watcher, it is being called a 'twitcher'. Except, of course, if they are actually on a 'twitch'. I'll explain the semantics of this, particularly for anybody who works in the local or national news media – the worst perpetrators of the 'twitcher' fallacy. Those of us who watch birds are properly called 'bird-watchers'; so far, so good. But there is a particular branch of bird-watching which goes by the name of 'twitching'. This is the pursuit of a particular rare bird, found by someone else and sometimes at great lengths, that one hasn't seen before or rarely sees. Naturally, for those bird-watchers who like to build a 'year list' – seeing the most species they can in one year – 'twitching' is a must. A further linguistic refinement has been to identify more closely those who might 'twitch', if the fancy took them, but generally enjoyed observing any species of bird – no matter how common – and their behaviour. Many, myself included, prefer to be identified as belonging to this last category, otherwise known as 'birders', which is really a more 'hip' word for bird-watcher. Right – that's all clear then.

I have twitched a lot myself, although I don't twitch much anymore, it has to be said, but there are a few birds I will travel out of my way to see. A wryneck is one of them.

For me, the wryneck is the epitome of what birders call a 'top bird'. It is quite simply a magnificent little creature that is, naturally, not easy to see being a classic 'skulker', often hiding from view. Appearing in Sussex and other, mostly coastal, parts of the country in the spring and autumn, it turns up on migration. The best time to look for wrynecks is in the autumn, particularly during September, and the best places to search are its favoured coastal haunts at Beachy Head as well as the area called the Severals, and the beach at Church Norton, Pagham Harbour.

As well as being difficult to see, an equally important part of the wryneck's charm is that it is also the 'king of weird'. Related to wood-peckers, at around 6-7 inches (16-18 cm) long the wryneck is about the size of a large warbler. Its markings are, er, remarkable. It is mainly mottled brown, but with a dark brown eye stripe, brown and grey stripes down its back, an ochrish-buff throat and a bright orange eye. And, while looking around on a perch, or on the ground, where it can be seen lurking and searching for food, it lengthens and twists its neck – hence the name wryneck. Its common nickname, 'snakebird', refers to its long, flickering tongue (useful for picking up ants, its main food) and hissing noise that it apparently makes if frightened on a nest.

Not that we get to see nest behaviour any more as they ceased to breed in Britain in 2003. Amazingly for what is now such a rare bird they were fairly common until the early 1900s. The wryneck last bred in Sussex in 1944 but stopped breeding regularly in the county in 1920, although Norman F. Ticehurst's *A History of the Birds of Kent* in 1909 describe the bird as 'plentiful and generally distributed throughout'. This reduction in numbers is presumed to have been caused by the inten-sification of agriculture, the loss of habitat and a decline in ants.

The ancient Greeks attributed all sorts of love-inducing mysticism to the bird to the extent of developing a dubious piece of technology called a 'wryneck wheel' – a hapless wryneck was trapped in a spinning wheel, where it was supposed to charm your favoured subject. Perhaps the wryneck's decline is the cause of there being a little less love in the world today. All you need is wrynecks.

Top Sites

◍ *Beachy Head, Cow Gap, August to September (see p.84)*   National grid ref. TV5995
◍ *Pagham Harbour August to September (see p.69)*   National grid ref. SZ8795

PART TWO

FAVOURITE SITES

A wildlife film cameraman once told me about a Canadian trapper he met, who had a deep understanding and love of the natural world he shared. To him it was so important, almost a ritual, to never name what he hoped to see. He would simply walk out each day with the expectation of only seeing what he was destined to see. That way, any creature that crossed his path gave him pleasure, providing a moment to be enjoyed in itself. It is a ritual I have – for most of the time – adopted, and which does seem to work in the sense that it encourages me to take pleasure in the world around me when out for a walk. Any rare bird that I chance upon is then a bonus.

But then again, even without the birds, those of us who are fortunate enough to spend much of our time outdoors in Sussex are able to experience a county that is rich in beautiful landscapes, from the Downs to the estuaries and marshes by the sea, from the heathlands and woods to the sweeping river valleys.

Here is my selection of just some of the places in Sussex where it is possible to enjoy birds and wildlife as well as, in many cases, some of the best scenery in the county. Further details, including contact numbers and websites of the organisations who run and maintain these sites, are listed on pages 88-9.

AMBERLEY WILD BROOKS

WINTER WONDERLAND

Each reserve has its own special character that changes through the season. Not exactly awash with birds, nevertheless, as I explain else-where, Waltham Brooks (*see p.82*) seems to draw me back time and again. However, with the potential for just as much, if not more, excite-ment are Waltham's neighbouring brooks, Amberley Wild Brooks, which border the Arun further downstream. Amberley has a completely different character and, especially during the winter, at the height of its attraction, a visit can provide a pretty tough day of bird-watching.

There are two reasons for this. It is a huge area and access is restricted to the long footpath, making it sometimes difficult to see all the birds hidden in the channels and pools of water. Secondly, especially in winter, the footpath can get very muddy indeed. It is this dampness that brings in large numbers of wintering ducks and waders, but can make a walk here heavy going. Yet it is as true of wildlife-watching as any other pursuit that success tastes all the sweeter for a little hardship. After all, we wouldn't want it to be too easy, would we?

Winter may not be the best time underfoot, but it is the best time for a walk at Amberley, especially if the brooks have been flooded by rain. Seen from the viewpoints on the Downs high above Amberley, the brooks along the valley can look like an immense inland lake. The attraction to wintering wildfowl, such as wigeon and teal, as well as hordes of lapwing (*see p.28*) and waders, is the food that the water and mud provide.

Also attracted to the flooded fields from time to time are beautiful Bewick's swans. These elegant birds come all the way from their breed-ing grounds in western Siberia. They are smaller than the mute swans that are present in the Arun Valley all year round, with a straighter neck and a blacker bill with distinctive yellow patches on the top of it.

To access Amberley Brooks, park by the Sussex Wildlife Trust's reserve at Waltham Brooks and, instead of walking out onto the SWT reserve, walk on the road over Greatham Bridge. As you cross the bridge, look up-stream in winter for Bewick's swans which sometimes feed on the fields here when they are flooded. After the bridge, turn right and walk along the footpath that starts along the east bank of the Arun. The path then climbs up through some trees – which can be good for woodpeckers, including the elusive lesser spotted woodpecker – past Quell Farm and a barn conversion, and into a small copse. The trees around here are meant to provide a home for the little owl, which feeds on worms and insects in the grass during the day, but they are not that easy to see. The path then takes you out onto the brooks. Barn owls (see p.14) also patrol this area all year, particularly towards dusk.

During a winter walk, watch the fields here for the vast flocks of lapwing, teal and wigeon rising into the air. The black clouds of birds moving and swaying across the sky may indicate that the birds have entered 'predator evasion' mode. They try to shake off a bird of prey by using their combined mass to distract it. Watch the birds carefully and you may be able to pick out a peregrine (see p.36) darting through the sky or, lower down, a large, elegant hen harrier (see p.24) quartering the fields. Short-eared owls (see p.40) are also regular visitors here most winters.

Seasonal highlights

◖ **Spring:** grasshopper warbler, Cetti's warbler, blackcap, cuckoo, garganey, hobby, common & green sandpipers

◖ **Summer:** cuckoo, Cetti's warbler

◖ **Autumn & winter:** Bewick's swan, short-eared owl, hen harrier, wigeon, pintail

◖ **All year:** barn owl

AMBERSHAM COMMON

MAGNIFICENT AMBERSHAM

We are very lucky to have such a range of healthy lowland heathland sites in Sussex, and around Petworth and Midhurst there is a line of particularly special commons that are home to Sussex's heathland specialities, and perhaps the best of these is Ambersham Common – or rather Ambersham and Heyshott Commons.

At most times of the year, these heathlands can seem a little dead, unless something of particular interest turns up, that is. By this, I mean a great grey shrike. The shrike is about the size of a blackbird and is known as 'the butcher bird' because of its not terribly nice habit of skewering its prey on the thorns of bushes for consumption at a later date. Looking like a huge finch with a long tail and heavy bill, the bird wears a distinctive black 'Zorro' mask across its face. The winter is also the time to look for, but not to expect, the sight of a hen harrier (*see p.24*) soaring over the heather and pines.

But it is the summer when the heathland commons come alive, and when I have to choose just one to visit, it is usually Ambersham Common. You can reach Ambersham by following the A272 west from Petworth and then taking the second left turning after Tillington. Follow the minor road south through South Ambersham, taking the left fork and continuing south along the narrow road until you begin climbing a hill with trees on your left and right. There is a small car park on your left not long after you enter the trees.

From here you can walk up a sandy hill, through the trees and onto Ambersham Common, surrounded by pines and a few lone trees. Stonechats will be obvious, flitting and calling around the bottom of the trees and over the heather. Linnets are also possible and, particularly in early spring, woodlarks (*see p.50*) will be calling from the trees around the north side of the common. At any time of year, crossbills might fly overhead in small parties, alighting to feed on the pine cones. The Dartford warblers (*see p.20*) will be present in and flitting over the heather, and should be obvious from their distinctive scratchy call.

Wait until dusk, though, for the nightjars (*see p.34*) and woodcock (*see p.48*). It is best to stand at the edges of the trees, or by one of the stands of pines, hiding your shape among the trees and waiting quietly. It's a good idea to bring a folding seat of some kind. The dark silhouettes of the woodcock will make their flights around the tops of the pines first. Waiting for the nightjars can seem like an eternity, punctuated by the irritation of midges, but it's always worth the wait. At first, you may think you've heard something, but aren't quite sure if you have. Then a distinctive, quiet churring will start up, sometimes seemingly close to your feet. At last, the nightjars will begin to fly, and you'll be alerted to their approach by the sharp '*kru-wick*' calls. With luck, you may even have close views, as I have had, of one churring from a branch.

On the western side of the road, footpaths sweep down to Heyshott Common, which is worth a mention as its vistas are good for spotting hen harriers in winter, hobbies (*see p.26*) in summer, and buzzards at any time of the year.

And one final word about visiting heathland on a summer's night. The nightjars love these places because of the large numbers of flies, moths and midges. Unfortunately, the midges are in turn big fans of human flesh, so cover yourself well and use whatever insect repellant you favour. Although you'd be well advised to avoid the stronger stuff as it can melt the plastic and rubber on expensive optical equipment.

Seasonal highlights

◄ *Spring & summer:* nightjar, woodlark, tree pipit, hobby, woodcock
◄ *Winter:* occasional hen harrier or great grey shrike, meadow pipit, fieldfare
◄ *All year:* Dartford warbler, stonechat, linnet, crossbill, siskin, redpoll, buzzard

ARUNDEL WILDFOWL & WETLANDS TRUST

ALONG THE BOARDWALK

Arundel's Wildfowl and Wetlands Trust visitor centre has excellent facilities, including a restaurant, shop, displays for children, and a level walkway that allows easy access for the elderly and people with pushchairs or wheelchairs. The walkways allow you to get really close views of the captive wildfowl and there's always something to see at any time of the year.

The Wildfowl and Wetlands Trust was founded by the late naturalist and artist Sir Peter Scott in 1946 and now has nine centres. A hero among conservationists, Scott had a vision for helping to preserve the world's wetlands that provide such important places for a range of wildlife, especially water birds. Today's visitor centres provide a place where people can see many endangered species, including the Hawaiian goose, which are bred in captivity to support reintroduction and conservation schemes.

Whatever the time of year, there is always something worth seeing, and the opportunity of observing at such close quarters birds that sometimes you only see very occasionally – such as long-tailed ducks – is not to be passed up.

Follow the walk round, past geese, swans and white-headed ducks and you'll come to some netted enclosures that are home to a few very rare, captive New Zealand blue ducks, special favourites of mine. Just around the corner is a small wooded area where there are some woodland birds, including nuthatches, treecreepers, woodpeckers, marsh tits and, of course, chaffinches and tits. The water around this area also holds some wild, breeding mandarin ducks.

The path leads off from here onto a boardwalk, which is a really exciting and, usually, quieter area of the reserve. The pools are great for dragonflies and damselflies in the summer, and this part is a reliable spot for the elusive water vole – which I consider an 'honorary bird' – although you'll need patience, and quiet. I've spotted them nibbling among the grassy fringes, just under the boardwalk here. Carry on round through the reeds, and you'll hear warblers, including Cetti's warblers (pronounced 'chetty's'), as well as reed buntings.

The boardwalk brings you back onto the path, where you can hear more Cetti's warblers (they are relatively common on this site) and which leads you to the wilder parts of the reserve. Here, hides over-look pools and rafts that have provided homes for nesting terns (*see p. 30*) and black-headed gulls in summer, and scrapes where you can spot green and common sandpipers in spring and autumn, and snipe in winter. The smaller jack snipe have even been spotted here in the winter. Flashing blue and orange kingfishers are regulars.

Winter is a great time to visit Arundel. The ducks are in their finest plumage (this is the time of year that they pair up), and the '*ooo-ooooh*' of the displaying male common eiders is a spectacle not to be missed. Watch out, especially on very cold days in midwinter, for water rails – long-billed marsh birds – so hard to see for the rest of the year, but for a few short, cold weeks they completely forget themselves and can be seen wandering in full view in the bird pens.

Also watch over the wooded hill called Offham Hanger (behind the visitor centre by the road) as often as you can, as there's always the chance of spotting a bird of prey soaring over the trees, as well as the rooks. Buzzards and peregrines (*see p. 36*) are regulars all year, hobbies (*see p. 26*) sometimes pass over and even honey buzzards and goshawks have been spotted.

Seasonal highlights

◀ *Spring & summer:* common tern, black-headed gull

◀ *Winter:* snipe, pochard, wigeon, water rail, very occasional bittern

◀ *All year:* peregrine falcon, buzzard, kingfisher, Cetti's warbler, chiffchaff,
   great spotted woodpecker, treecreeper, nuthatch, marsh tit, grey wagtail

ASHDOWN FOREST

HEATHLAND HEAVEN

Ashdown Forest is an emerald jewel in the heart of Sussex. Covering 6,500 acres (2,500 hectares) – two-thirds of which are heathland – the Forest offers a sprawling network of woods, heaths, fields and scrub, as well as beautiful scenery, with views across the Weald down to the sea, shimmering in the distance.

The Forest has been used for hunting, grazing and iron-working, but it has never been cultivated. The word 'forest' actually comes from the Latin *foris* meaning 'outside' and this applied to areas that belonged to the Crown and were set aside for hunting outside the areas available for cultivation. The royal hunting grounds at Ashdown were handed down through various aristocratic hands for hundreds of years. It was only in 1988 that East Sussex County Council bought the Forest from the Earl de la Warr's estate and established the Ashdown Forest Trust as its owner. Today, the Forest is one of the largest spaces offering free public access in the south-east of England and exploring the wildlife-rich woods and heathland never fails to fill me with wonder.

Turn up on a bustling weekend in May with busy roads and car parks crowded with people, children and dogs, and it may be a little difficult to conjure up a sense of wonder at all. But persistence pays. Find your way to one of the key car parks and go for a walk and it is possible to find peace, quiet, great views and lots of good birds and other wildlife. Of course, in what was once a royal hunting forest, there are still plenty of deer. As well as the roe and fallow deer, there are a few of the smaller sika and the tiny, dog-like muntjac deer wandering around, but these tend to be shy.

The Ashdown Forest Centre, 1 mile (1.6 km) east of the traffic lights at Wych Cross, is a good place to begin as it provides an outline of the history and wildlife of the Forest. A summer evening visit, however, after the centre has closed, is the best time to visit for the birds. The heathland to the north is a good place to watch for woodcock (*see p.48*) and nightjar (*see p.34*). The woodcock emerge first, before dusk, so listen for their peculiar calls. The nightjars will begin to churr around dusk and, if you're lucky, you'll see them fly past and display. You'll also hear the calls of tawny owls echoing from the trees.

Gills Lap is an area of heathland, with occasional pines and gorse, that is perfect for Dartford warblers (*see p.20*). It is also the area most associated with A.A. Milne's *Winnie the Pooh* and so it attracts a lot of visitors. Given the popularity of the spot, it takes a little patience to see Dartford warblers, but the key is to listen for their scratchy bursts of song. A bit of warmth and sunshine – and peace and quiet – will entice them up to sing from the top of the heather and gorse. This can also be a good area for the occasional wintering great grey shrike. For Gills Lap, follow the road east from the Ashdown Forest Centre, taking the next turn right and park at one of the car parks by the fork in the road.

Other good spots for woodcock and nightjar, known as the Isle of Thorns and the Old Airstrip, are accessible by driving south-east from Wych Cross traffic lights, along the A22, and parking in the Long Park car park. Walk south from here through the trees and out onto the heathland. The evening hours before dusk may provide views of redpolls coming in to roost and you will also hear the '*chuck-whirr*' mutterings of Dartford warblers from the heather and gorse.

Another good place to find redpolls is in the trees around Ellison's Pond. From Long Park, drive south along the A22 and take the next left along the minor road heading east and park in one of the two car parks on the left. It is also possible to walk north from here and down to the stream at Old Lodge Bottom. The trees here hold redstarts, warblers, tits and woodpeckers. The nearby gorse on the slopes is home to more Dartford warblers.

South of Ellison's Pond is Airman's Grave, where the Forest opens up to reveal magnificent vistas across the South Downs to the sea and you can watch for hobbies (*see p.26*) and buzzards (*see p.18*) soaring in the sky.

One of my favourite walks in the Forest is around the Sussex Wildlife Trust's Old Lodge Nature Reserve. A summer visit will never disappoint. Take the trail through the varied habitats of acid grassland, pines and heather and you will stand a good chance of seeing a range of wildlife, including silver-studded blue butterflies, black darters and golden-ringed dragonflies around the specially dug ponds, adders and of course the grazing Exmoor ponies – not wildlife, but charming animals, nonetheless.

The birds you can see in this area include the pretty, soft-grey spotted flycatcher, leaping from its tree to catch insects and returning to its perch again. This is also a great place to see displaying tree pipit, redpoll and, a personal favourite, woodlark (*see p.50*). We have enjoyed some really close views of woodlark feeding along the edge of the stands of pines. The trees also provide excellent homes for breeding common redstarts. These beautiful little birds – they look rather like elongated robins (they are related to robins) with black faces and a white brow, grey backs and rusty red underparts – aren't all that common in the south of England now. In 2006, it was estimated that there were around 55 pairs in Sussex, as indicated by the singing males, and 44 of these were to be found in Ashdown Forest (most at Pippingford Park and Old Lodge). As with many woodland birds, it pays to listen for its song first to be able to track it down – a short, sad '*see-truee-truee-truee*'.

Bird-watching in woodland or heathland can be frustrating – sometimes you think you've strayed into a bird-free zone – but as I said at the outset, perseverance pays. If you are unfamiliar with Ashdown Forest, the complex plethora of sites and interconnecting walks may seem daunting. Indeed, it would take a lifetime to get to know the area well, but it is this large choice of places to visit and things to see that draws me back time and again.

Seasonal highlights

- *Spring & summer:* nightjar, woodlark, common redstart, tree pipit, spotted flycatcher, hobby, woodcock
- *Winter:* hen harrier, great grey shrike
- *All year:* Dartford warbler, stonechat, meadow pipit, skylark, crossbill, siskin, redpoll, woodcock, buzzard

BURTON MILL & CHINGFORD PONDS

PEACE AND PONDLIFE

There are some places where it doesn't really matter if you don't see any birds at all; they are so lovely and peaceful that they replenish your soul. Such is the importance of wild places and why it is essential for our society that we continue to value them and support organisations like the Wildlife Trusts, who quietly and diligently preserve them for all of us. Burton Mill Pond is just such a place.

Take the A285 south out of Petworth, over the Coultershaw Bridge, by the beam pump, and take the next left. After about 1 mile (1.6 km), turn left just before Burton Mill Pond down into a small car park. It is possible to take an excellent 2-mile (3-km) circular walk around the reserve, passing through a range of different habitats. But first, whatever the season, cross the road, through the gate and enjoy the sight of the reed-fringed Burton Mill Pond. It is such a lovely spot that it is hard to believe it was once the scene of a bustling Sussex industry. This was a 16th-century hammer pond, which was used to feed pumps that powered an iron forge.

Today, in the summer, reed warblers chatter along the edges, close to your feet. Great crested grebes are often serenely gliding and feeding, along with squabbling coots, and a kingfisher may whirr across the water. A hobby (*see p.26*) might pass overhead, hawking for insects. In the winter, the pond attracts good numbers of tufted duck, gadwall, shoveler and pochard. Bitterns (*see p.16*) also occasionally drop in during the winter, and I've watched them fishing in the evening light on the other side of the pond.

Take the footpath onto the reserve proper, through a gate. Turn left by the tall pine trees, watching for siskin, redpoll and marsh tit. This looped footpath takes you past the edge of the pond, and provides a good look-out point across the water. The path loops round through damp alder woodland, or carr as it's called, and it's in among all this dense stuff that you can sometimes hear – and more rarely see – the lesser spotted woodpecker. Its name is appropriate as it's rarely spotted by anyone these days. But the walk here is one of the best places to look for them in late February and March. As always, listen for the sound first: its call is a high-pitched '*pee-pee-pee*'; and its drumming is feint, in longer but weaker bursts than the great spotted woodpecker's, but difficult to identify positively. You're looking for a small bird, roughly the size of a great tit, that looks similar to but a little more dumpy than its larger cousin.

The footpath continues round to Chingford Pond, which is also the result of human digging, but this time for the purposes of landscaping rather than industry. It is good for ducks, kingfishers, little egrets and common and green sandpipers in spring and autumn, and the occasional bittern in winter. The damp woodland to the north is again a good spot to look or listen for lesser spotted woodpeckers.

Turning east, then north, the path takes you through conifers, where the high-pitched calls of siskin and goldcrest can fill the air around you. The path finally leads down to a very rare but pretty unprepossessing habitat of peat bog known as the 'black hole'. The Sussex Wildlife Trust has done a lot of clearing work here to allow bogbean, white sedge and yellow loosestrife to thrive once again and also to encourage dragonflies, such as the golden-ringed, scarce chaser, downy emerald, black-tailed skimmer and emperor.

The path eventually comes out onto a heathland area good for adders and lizards, and then to the road, which loops back round to the mill and car park.

Seasonal highlights

- *Spring & summer:* hobby, reed warbler, great crested grebe
- *Winter:* pochard, tufted duck, siskin, redpoll, occasional bittern
- *Spring & autumn:* passing common and green sandpipers
- *All year:* kingfisher, lesser and greater spotted woodpeckers, goldcrest, crossbill, little owl, grey wagtail, mandarin duck, little egret, common buzzard, water rail, little grebe

CUCKMERE HAVEN

MEADOWS, MEANDERS & MORE

In the dip in the coast between the white cliffs of the Seven Sisters to the east and Seaford Head to the west lies the bay of Cuckmere Haven, the mouth of the canalised River Cuckmere. The picture-postcard views of the white cliffs of the Seven Sisters draw many visitors to the area, but there are good bird-watching reasons to come here as well.

To access the area north of the river, park at Seven Sisters Country Park visitor centre on the A259, then walk west to Exceat Bridge by the Golden Galleon pub. Just before the bridge, a footpath leads north along the east side of the river. The water meadows here are a great place in winter to look for geese, including white-fronted geese, bean geese, pink-footed geese, or even barnacle geese. The seagulls that regularly haunt the fields can include Mediterranean gull. Riverside bushes hold migrants in spring and autumn, including warblers and ring ouzel.

South of the road, a path by the Golden Galleon car park leads down to the marsh on the west side of the canal. The fields and scrub hold passing warblers in spring and autumn, as well as whitethroat and lesser whitethroat. The raised hedge across the middle of the marsh is a favourite roost of grey heron and little egret. Wintering duck paddle around down in the ditches, but the lapwing (*see p.28*) and geese should be more obvious, and a passing bird of prey may scare everything skywards. Keep your ears open for the whistle of a kingfisher flashing along the canal, or the '*veesst*' call of a rock pipit. Redshank and dunlin will frequent the muddy sides of the river at low tide.

Back at the visitor centre, on the east side of the river, paths lead down past the meanders to the canal, a small 'wader scrape' and the sea. Again, waterfowl will be prevalent in winter, along with little grebe, little egret, lapwing and cormorant. Waders such as redshank, dunlin and ringed plover roost on the far muddy riverbank, and greenshank and curlew sandpiper are possible here in autumn. Little egret, gulls, godwits and knot frequent the wader scrape and the nearby scrub is good for passing migrants. Sea birds are often too far out for sea watching, but the wintering red-throated diver is a regular. Look up at the cliffs in the summer for nesting fulmar and regular peregrine falcon (*see p. 36*).

If the Seven Sisters are an iconic image, then so are the 'meanders' that give the Cuckmere its local name of 'snake river'. The meanders are no longer a flowing part of the river, as the canal and its banks were built to prevent flooding, but rising seas mean that they are more and more difficult and expensive to maintain. The Environment Agency now plans to allow the marsh on the west side of the river to flood and revert to estuarine mud flats. The meanders would be reconnected to the water flow and allowed to function again as before. At the time of writing, no final decision had been reached but some locals are concerned at the proposed changes to this popular landscape, even though it will be allowed essentially to change naturally again. Whatever happens to the Cuckmere will be a case study in how we manage our coastlines for wildlife and people in the face of rising water levels.

The changes will undoubtedly benefit wildlife, with large numbers of waders being attracted to any new mud flats. Footpaths further up the sides of the valley will be created to allow viewing of the area, if not access.

Seasonal highlights

◄ *Spring:* whimbrel, warblers

◄ *Summer:* lesser and common whitethroat, fulmar

◄ *Autumn:* occasional avocet, occasional black- and bar-tailed godwits, knot, curlew sandpiper, greenshank

◄ *Winter:* golden plover, red-throated diver, Mediterranean gull, occasional white-fronted, bean, pink-footed or barnacle geese

◄ *All year:* peregrine, rock pipit, little egret, lapwing, redshank, dunlin, little grebe, kingfisher, stonechat, occasional raven

PAGHAM HARBOUR

WATERFOWL, WADERS & WRYNECKS

As East Sussex has Rye Harbour (*see p. 77*), so West Sussex has Pagham Harbour. The symmetry is a pleasing and fortunate one for those who live either so far to the west or so far to the east of Sussex that a trip to one becomes quite an expedition. Pagham Harbour has probably been one of my favourite places to watch birds ever since I first came to Sussex. I still feel a sense of freedom and anticipation every time I stand on the shingle spit near Church Norton, surveying the vast tidal mud flats, salt marsh, muddy pools and inlets that attract so many birds all year.

Get the timing and the tide right and you can see a good range of waders, sea birds, ducks, geese, even a passing bird of prey or rare migrant. Although some things can be difficult to see – never expect wildlife to just 'perform' to order for you – you really don't need to walk far, or look hard to see something that will make your day. On the other hand, I like oystercatchers a lot, they're always so bright and cheerful to see, a sort of poor man's puffin, so I'm probably more easily pleased than most.

Pagham Harbour, as its name implies, hasn't always been so peaceful or wildlife friendly as it is today. In the 12th and 13th centuries, it was one of the most important ports in the country, shipping wool abroad, until a massive storm put paid to all that. The sea engulfed the port, submerged the hamlet of Charlton, the harbour silted up and the port went into a decline and had all but ceased to exist by 1400. However, nature abhors a vacuum, and so it was that, when the busy harbour became silted up with mud, the birds moved in.

The area of the Harbour is vast, but there are footpaths and access points. I tend to divide the Harbour up into three large areas, and pick which of the three I want to park near or walk to depending on the weather, season, time available and news of what is around.

Firstly, there's the visitor centre and the Sidlesham Ferry Pool area, at the western, inland corner of the harbour. This is a good place to stop for news and information and toilets. Walk south from the car park, past some bushes – which offer shelter to small migrants and linnets – to a hide which overlooks the B2154. Beyond the road is the Ferry Pool. Morning to midday is really the best time to look here as the sun is rising behind you. In the spring or autumn, you may see a collection of various interesting waders, including stints, sandpipers, godwits and ruff, or ducks, such as garganey; winter is a good time for other sheltering wildfowl. Witnessing the annual influx of curlew sandpiper – little waders similar to dunlin with decurved bills – in the autumn, usually September, is always a favourite pilgrimage. The Ferry Pool is a well-known spot for some extremely rare birds stopping over in spring or autumn, so it's always worth a look.

From the hide, walk south and cross the sluice. The muddy channel that leads towards the harbour is good for redshank. Walk east along the right side of the Long Pool. This reed-fringed stretch of water is good for little grebe, reed bunting and reed warbler in the spring and summer. To the right is an area of farmland where you can see grey partridge (*see p.22*), meadow pipit, skylark (*see p.42*), curlew or even a short-eared owl (*see p.40*) quartering the fields in winter.

The path leads along the southern edge of the mud flats, all along to another hide and the next main birding area by Church Norton. You can, however, drive further south along the B2154, taking the next left up a lane that leads to the church car park. From the car park it is a short walk past the old Norman castle ditches and mounds, and past tall trees down to a brackish pool (listen and watch for woodpeckers and blackcaps, and redstarts or flycatchers passing through in spring or autumn). This pool is a great spot for waders such as curlew, redshank or oystercatcher, or a little egret, and you can get some really close views here.

The mud banks, inland from the shingle spit that stretches across the mouth of the harbour, are good places to spot ringed plover, dunlin, turnstone, and in spring a special treat is seeing hosts of newly arrived grey plover looking self-important and spectacular in their pale grey 'judge's wig' plumage. It is always worth scanning the islands – a pale glaucous gull might turn up in winter and I have also seen a resting peregrine (*see p.36*) a couple of times. You should see a few terns in this area in spring and summer including little tern (*see p.30*) which are breeding on the beach again. Remember to watch the skies for passing birds of prey, a clue to their presence being the clouds of waders and starlings that soar up in terror. At high tide in winter, the pools can be good for sheltering divers, grebes or even guillemot.

To visit the other side of the harbour, or North Wall area, and Pagham Lagoon, you can take the path that leads north from the visitor centre, along the northern edges of the marsh, through the bushes that might hold something special in spring or autumn, or you can take your car and park by Pagham Spit. Passing black redstart and wheatear turn up in spring and rock pipit are regular along the water's edge. A mile's walk inland from the Spit is the North Wall area, from where you can look for geese and curlew and at the Breech Pool you may see reed warbler and possibly garganey and water rail.

Finally, I must mention Pagham beach and the area of scrub and bushes between the beach and the inland pools known as the Severals. On the beach, there can be small flocks of waders feeding along the water's edge. Winter is a good time to look for rare grebes, particularly Slavonian, or divers offshore and, very occasionally, you can also pick up twite or snow bunting here. However, for me the biggest draw is the potential for something even more special – a wryneck (*see p.52*). Autumn is the time when wrynecks might appear and you'll only have to follow the other birders to find these birds, but look for them skulking around the Severals. The wrynecks, that is.

Seasonal highlights

◄ **Spring:** *flycatcher, redstart, wheatear, common, little and sandwich tern, whimbrel, willow warbler, blackcap, grey plover, rare waders*

◄ **Summer:** *spotted flycatcher, terns, including breeding little tern, reed warbler*

◄ **Autumn:** *curlew sandpiper, spotted redshank, wryneck, flycatcher, passing birds of prey*

◄ **Winter:** *Slavonian grebe, hen harrier, short-eared owl, glaucous gull, rock pipit, twite*

PETT LEVEL & RYE BAY

POOLS, A CANAL & THE SEA

Just south of Winchelsea, at the south-west end of Rye Harbour lies Rye Bay and behind it, behind the sea wall, are Pett Pools and the Pett Level Local Nature Reserve. Access to the Bay and Pett Level is by following the Pett Level Road through Winchelsea Beach from the east, or following the minor road off the A259 from Hastings in the east. You can park anywhere along the coast road which runs in the shadow of the sea wall.

The elevated sea wall was a defence built in 1940 and now provides a useful place to stand and watch Pett Pools, north of the road. The Pools host a variety of waders, particularly on passage in spring and autumn, including spotted redshank, both black-tailed and bar-tailed godwits, dunlin, sandpipers (including curlew sandpiper), ringed plover, stints (with an occasional Temminck's) and avocet. Birds of prey that might happen to be around are passing marsh harrier or peregrine falcon. Out on the fields, wintering greylag and Canada geese can be joined by white-fronted, pink-footed and even barnacle geese.

Turning around to face the sea – if the weather permits – you can watch for birds on the water in winter, such as grebe, red-throated diver and common scoter. Looking at the common scoter flocks very carefully through the telescope may even reveal a velvet scoter – distinguishable from its jet black common cousins by its white eye and wing patches and the larger patch of yellow on its bill. During the summer, you'll hear the sharp cries of terns, including sandwich, common and little, as they fly along the coast to and from their nests on the Rye Harbour reserve, sometimes hovering and diving as they fish for food.

Below you, on the beach, you should spot turnstones, and at low tide the cheerful-chappy oystercatchers will be ever-present, together with dunlin, redshank, curlew and sometimes grey plover.

An interesting feature of the muddy beach revealed at low tide is the 'moorlog' – the fossilised remains of an ancient forest, complete with prone tree trunks, that dates back to before the last Ice Age, around 6,000 years ago.

Turning your attention back inland, and to more recent times, the Royal Military Canal stretches inland before jinking right, level with the line of the coast. The canal was built between 1804 and 1809, during the Napoleonic Wars, as part of the programme to construct defences in the face of the very real threat of French invasion. The idea was that the canal would obstruct any attempt to move large forces inland. These days it provides a peaceful and ironic sanctuary for wildlife. You can walk by the canal, along the Saxon Shore Way, from the western end of the sea wall to Pett Level, and back across the reserve to the sea wall, where you might just spot a snow bunting in the winter.

Where the canal turns right, there are a couple of bridges across the river into the Pannel Valley reserve, which consists of reed and marsh and a little scrape. Summer here brings cuckoo, whitethroat and warblers and, again, a marsh harrier might be spotted in winter.

Seasonal highlights

- *Spring:* spotted redshank, black- and bar-tailed godwits, dunlin, sandpipers (including curlew sandpiper), ringed plover, stints (occasional Temminck's), little ringed plover, whimbrel, avocet, garganey, chiffchaff, blackcap, wheatear
- *Summer:* reed and sedge warblers, little, sandwich and common terns, cuckoo, whitethroat
- *Autumn:* occasional marsh harrier, hobby, spotted redshank
- *Winter:* hen harrier, rock pipit, occasional snow bunting, red-throated diver, common eider, common scoter, occasional velvet scoter
- *All year:* peregrine, barn owl, lapwing, curlew, redshank, dunlin, little egret, kingfisher

PULBOROUGH BROOKS

JEWEL OF THE ARUN

My career as a birder is inextricably linked to the RSPB reserve of Pulborough Brooks. It was here that my keen interest in birds and wildlife turned into a more substantial passion. On our very first visit, many years ago, while walking down to West Mead hide, we saw a short-eared owl (see p.40) fly across the field in front of us, and Pulborough Brooks has been an important part of our birding life ever since.

You can find Pulborough Brooks by following the A283 south of Pulborough, heading towards Storrington. The reserve is very popular on sunny days and the car park has been expanded to accommodate the higher than average footfall. With a shop, tearoom and toilet facilities, Pulborough is one of the RSPB's 'flagship' reserves.

Birding begins in the car park at Pulborough, with nuthatch being a regular in the trees by the visitor centre – listen for its tell-tale, loud and repeated, rising '*chu-eet*' call and look for a small blue and orange woodpecker-like bird shinning along the branches of the mature trees. Even the lesser spotted woodpecker has been seen among these trees and on the feeders in February and March. This is a bird that has become almost mythical as a result of its increasing rarity.

The woods behind the car parks on Wiggonholt Common harbour woodlark (see p.50), woodcock (see p.48) and some nightjar (see p.34) in the summer and, very rarely, roaming flocks of crossbill and redpoll. The RSPB has been restoring this area – once heavily planted with conifers – to its former heathland and woodland splendour. Thanks to this work, woodlark have returned to breed and it is hoped that Dartford warblers (see p.20) will soon follow suit.

The way to the reserve is through the shop, where you pay or show your RSPB membership card. At times when the centre is closed, however, you can gain entry through a side gate. Even the visitor centre has held barn owls (*see p.14*) in a nest box up in the roof above the tearoom. The owls nest there regularly, so if you are wandering about the centre on a summer's evening, please do be quiet and careful as you walk past, so that you do not disturb any nesting birds.

The footpath leads out onto the top of a field, where a pond and some scrub have been left to encourage small birds, and it's worth pausing to take in the magnificent view across the brooks. The field attracts green woodpeckers all year and whitethroat adopt the scrub in summer, but in winter this is a good spot for thrushes, such as fieldfare and redwing, and flocks of finches and buntings, including goldfinch, greenfinch, yellowhammer and sometimes corn bunting. The crop in the field is on rotation, so if it is sown in the spring and left for stubble in the winter, small farmland birds are drawn to it for food and shelter – an exemplary demonstration of what they need in winter on the surrounding farmland but are increasingly denied.

The path leads down the hill. The tall trees and hedge to the side shelter calling yellowhammer, woodpeckers and finches. At the bottom of the hill, the group of pines holds goldcrest, and crossbill and redpoll have been known to pass through.

The pond just after the conifers, and sheltered by mature oaks, is a regular spot for nightingale (*see p.32*). This is also an excellent spot for nuthatch and for lesser spotted woodpecker. The pretty songs of blackcaps can be heard in the surrounding bushes and trees in the spring and summer.

After the old oaks, the path turns to the left and to the right. Many people don't bother turning left, and head off to the right, to climb over the hill that leads to the Hanger and Nettley's hides. However, it isn't a long walk round the reserve, and I hate to think I might be missing anything, so I tend to do the 'whole loop' anyway.

The truth to tell, the West Mead hide rarely has anything remarkable in front of it – just the occasional black-winged stilt, common crane or spoonbill to name a few in recent years. Okay, they're not always there, but never discount the possibility. More likely are kestrel and buzzard, sandpiper and snipe if the water levels are right, as well as shoveler and shelduck. You may see the dark fallow deer that feed on the reserve. The path then winds on to the Winpenny hide. This is usually fairly quiet, although you should get good views of lapwing (*see p.28*) at any time of the year, and a kingfisher may zip by once in a while. Some visits to this hide, particularly when the fields are flooded in winter, can be staggering. I remember watching a formation hunting team of short-eared owls here one New Year's Day.

Walking on around the reserve brings you to Little Hanger hide, which can be good for snipe and golden plover in the muddy margins of the grass, but I prefer to stop at the open Hanger hide. This commands excellent vistas over the muddy pools of the Brooks and has been where I have seen hunting peregrine (*see p.36*), as well as feeding garganey in spring and golden plover among the lapwing in autumn. During the winter, however, when the brooks are heavily flooded, the elevated position of this hide is the best place to appreciate the spectacle of thousands of wintering wigeon, gadwall, pintail, teal and lapwing, and to watch for hunting peregrine or wintering hen harrier (*see p.24*). The dense thickets around Little Hanger are also among the key spots on the reserve to listen for singing nightingale in the spring.

From here, you can walk down through the trees to Nettley's hide. The wooded walk can reveal treecreeper, but the best time to look for them is definitely in the early morning, before too many people have passed. And Nettley's can get crowded, as most people head for this hide. It's not surprising that they do, as it's possible to get quite close to water rail, moving in front of the hide, and to enjoy a little closer up the spectacle of wintering duck. Don't forget to scan the fence posts for raptors – usually revealed by exciteable lapwing – and in the summer, look for hobbies (*see p.26*) hawking for insects and hirundines (members of the swallow family) over the water.

Seasonal highlights
◀ **Spring & summer:** nightingale, blackcap, whitethroat, cuckoo, garganey, hobby
◀ **Autumn:** common, green and wood sandpipers
◀ **Winter:** Bewick's swan, short-eared owl, hen harrier, wigeon, pintail, ruff, snipe, dunlin
◀ **All year:** peregrine, barn owl, little egret, lapwing, nuthatch, treecreeper, lesser spotted woodpecker, yellowhammer, bullfinch

RYE HARBOUR NATURE RESERVE

THE SHINGLE LIFE

Rye was once a large and important sea port; so important that the French and Spanish regularly raided the town. The original port is now 2 miles (3.2 km) inland, the sea having deposited great lumps of shingle onto the shore over 500 years. Camber Castle, built by Henry VIII on a shingle spit to defend Rye is now 1¼ miles (2 km) inland. Today, the invasions are much more peaceful and, being of the feathered variety, much more pleasurable for the bird-watcher.

Rye Harbour's varying habitats cover what is essentially the under-lying shingle, with the older shingle, further inland, being more heavily vegetated. These unusual and harsh conditions mean that many rare and endangered plants and animals are found in the area. The large gravel pits left by shingle extraction also attract a range of wildlife, including many birds that come to nest on the reserve during the summer, stop over on passage in spring and autumn or spend the winter here. A day's list of birds seen (or heard) at Rye can number into the 70s! Virtually any time of year is a good time to visit.

To reach the reserve, park in the free car park at the end of Harbour Road, by the 19th-century Martello tower fortification. From here, you can take a number of routes which lead out to several areas on the reserve, and you can organise your day around one or more of these areas.

By taking the track that leads beside the River Rother, you first come to the Lime Kiln Cottage visitor centre. The salt marsh behind the centre is good for meadow pipits in summer and rock pipits in winter.

A little closer to the sea and on your right is a remnant of salt marsh at the Wader Pool, preserved by the controlled flooding of sea water, and redshank are present here all year. The large Colin Green hide is a good place to take shelter and watch for ringed plover, oystercatcher, avocet and lapwing (*see p.28*). Stretching into the distance in front of you is the Flat Beach – a huge field of shingle where you can often see large flocks of golden plover in winter and other waders such as spotted redshank. If you walk on towards the sea, you may see eider or rare grebes on the water, or passing scoter. In summer, if it is warm and sunny, the heat haze can make seeing anything on the ground very difficult.

Just to your right, as you walk south along the beach road, is the Beach Reserve that stretches down to Winchelsea Beach. Little terns (see p. 30) have nested here and in a fenced off area on the shingle bank to the left, but recent years have seen a sad decline in breeding numbers to the extent that this sweet little bird – whose image is used as the symbol of the reserve – did not breed here in 2007 and 2008.

A path leads inland to the New Parkes hide that overlooks the Ternery Pool. There is a large black-headed gull colony here. Little grebe and tufted duck swim around in front of the hide. To make up for the disappointment of the decline of breeding little terns, handsome Mediterranean gulls have begun to breed here – 60 pairs nesting in 2008. Slightly larger and nobler looking than the black-headed gulls, they have a blacker head, a bright red bill and white 'eyelashes' above and below their eyes. Outside the hide, you can look back at the Quarry, a flooded pool, the margins of which can be good for all sorts of waders.

You can either follow the path and head back to the car park from here or head back to the road and continue south. Turning back onto the beach road takes you down to the Crittall hide which also overlooks the Ternery Pool. From here you can see the nesting sandwich and common terns which fly to and from the sea noisily during the summer. This is also a good place to spot passing waders, such as greenshank, ruff and sandpipers in autumn, or wintering duck.

Back on the road, you can walk over the bank of shingle that separates – and attempts to hold at bay – the sea from the reserve. Turnstone, dunlin, curlew, grey plover and knot can also turn up on the shore.

It's a long walk down, past the old lifeboat house, but finally you'll reach the point at which the path heads inland to the bottom of Long Pit. This is a great place to look in winter for duck, such as smew and goldeneye, or rare grebes, including red-necked and black-necked. The walk north passes the Harbour Farm barns, where you can see yellow wagtail, turtle dove and corn bunting in the summer, and takes you back to the Harbour Road and the car park.

From the bottom of Long Pit, you can also take the footpath that leads straight inland, past scrub (good for Cetti's warblers) and into a wooded area, where you'll find chiffchaff, woodpeckers, chaffinch and tits. Following the footpath north, through muddy fields and past grazing cattle, will take you to the area around Camber Castle and to the hide overlooking Castle Water. From there you'll see Mediterranean gull, black-headed gull and common tern in the summer, waders on passage and wintering duck, grebes, red-throated diver, or even a bittern in winter. Cetti's warblers also explode into song in the bushes outside the hide and in the gorse further south.

The fields around Camber Castle are good for lapwing, curlew and barn owl (*see p.14*). A footpath leads back past Castle Water to Harbour Road, and back to the car park.

Just before you reach the road, at the top end of the vast network of pools and reedbed that make up Castle Water, is an access path to a raised wooden platform. This viewpoint is popular in winter because of its regular dusk shows of bitterns (*see p.16*) flying back to their roosts. As many as half a dozen have been seen in one evening as they flew over and dropped down into the reeds. It also provides an excellent look-out for spotting bearded tit, marsh harrier, barn owl, little egret and hearing water rail or Cetti's warbler, depending on the season.

Seasonal highlights

◀ *Spring & summer:* wheatear, little, sandwich and common terns, Mediterranean gull, little ringed plover, whimbrel, avocet, garganey, chiffchaff, blackcap, corn bunting, reed and sedge warblers, turtle dove, occasional marsh harrier, hobby

◀ *Spring & autumn:* golden plover, black-tailed and bar-tailed godwits, curlew sandpiper, spotted redshank, little stint, black redstart, bearded tit, marsh harrier

◀ *Winter:* hen harrier, rock pipit, smew, red-throated diver, goldeneye, spotted redshank, common eider

◀ *All year:* barn owl, lapwing, curlew, redshank, dunlin, turnstone, Cetti's warbler, water rail, little egret, kingfisher, common scoter

THORNEY ISLAND

ISLAND PARADISE

A trip to Thorney Island is definitely an adventure, and not one for those of a nervous disposition or weak legs – or with a file held by MI5, probably. Thorney Island is a promontory that sticks out into Chichester Harbour and is not the easiest site to access. But remember, none but the brave deserve the fair. In spring and autumn, a majestic osprey could turn up anywhere around the area, resting on a post or flying overhead.

Park in nearby Emsworth, west of Chichester along the A259. Walk south, past the marina, and out onto the sea wall that borders Thorney Island. To the west and south are the muddy gullies that lead to the Emsworth Channel where it's always worth looking out for Mediterranean gull and red-breasted merganser in winter, and whimbrel and black-tailed godwit in spring or autumn. As you walk south, you'll see the Deeps on your left – a Local Nature Reserve. The scrub around the first area of water, called Little Deep holds Cetti's warbler – given away by their offensive-sounding splutterings – and the areas of water hold ducks and little grebe, while the reeds can shelter bearded tit. Further south, the muddy patches on the edge of the channel known as Great Deep are renowned for the numbers of waders that can build up here in autumn, including greenshank.

The centre of Thorney Island belongs to the Ministry of Defence and trespass is punishable by death, or similar. Even access to the sea wall is restricted. At the gate, you simply press the buzzer and wait for a response. You then look at the camera, give your name and address and, before you have time to worry about whether that parking ticket really does warrant a trip to Guantanamo Bay, you're in.

As you walk south, keeping to the sea wall, check the water for wintering duck. Considering the James Bond-style access arrangements, the appropriately named goldeneye are winter regulars here, and very occasionally long-tailed duck. Back inland, snipe wander about in the winter and grey partridge (*see p.22*) are regularly seen here. After turning south-east at Marker Point, look inland in winter for brent geese and possibly short-eared owl (*see p.40*) and golden plover around the airfield.

Once you finally reach Longmere Point on the south-easternmost part of the promontary, you'll be relieved to know that there's a hide overlooking the RSPB reserve at Pilsey Island, just offshore, and that you're about halfway round. Don't be too relieved, though – there are no toilets – but at least it's somewhere to sit down. Try to get the tide right for your stop-over here – you'll want it to be as near to a high tide as possible, or just before. High tide brings in many roosting waders, including dunlin, knot, sanderling, bar-tailed godwit and ringed plover in winter and curlew sandpiper and little stint in autumn. There's also the chance of corn bunting on the island in winter. Don't forget to watch the surrounding water for grebe and merganser.

And then it's the long, and usually in winter pretty muddy, walk back north along the eastern edge of the Thorney Island, past West Thorney and its church, and through another gate. On your right, the mud flats either side of Thorney Channel can hold more waders. Follow the path back to Emsworth, along the northern edge of the Deeps reserve. The late afternoon is a good time to watch for barn and short-eared owls over the fields in autumn or winter – a fitting end to what was hopefully an exhilarating and bird-filled 6-mile (10-km) walk.

Seasonal highlights

- *Spring: osprey, hobby, whimbrel*
- *Summer: terns (including little tern), turtle dove*
- *Autumn: osprey, hobby, curlew sandpiper, little stint*
- *Winter: short-eared and barn owls, red-breasted merganser, Slavonian grebe, avocet, knot, sanderling, greenshank, snipe, eider, very occasional long-tailed duck*
- *All year: Cetti's warbler, bearded tit, grey partridge, black-tailed godwit, little egret, Mediterranean gull, peregrine*

WALTHAM BROOKS

THE COMPANY OF WARBLERS

It is sometimes difficult to say why a particular place draws you back to it again and again, but there is often something intangible, undefinable about the pull of a special place except that you feel at peace, and somehow more complete when you're there. For me, Waltham Brooks is just such a place.

Just down the road from the RSPB's Pulborough Brooks (*see p.74*), Waltham Brooks is a small reserve tended by the Sussex Wildlife Trust. Take the A29 from Pulborough and then the minor road east in Coldwaltham across the railway bridge and turn right into the small car park just before Greatham Bridge.

Before walking out onto the reserve, take a walk up to the bridge and look up-river, towards Pulborough. The open fields here usually contain a few lapwing '*pee-woo-opping*' (*see p.28*) and in winter, you might see a few Bewick's swans wandering about the shallow pools. The river here is always worth a look. I've seen beautifully marked grass snakes – with their black stripes and alert yellow and black eyes – swimming along the Arun, and this is also a reliable spot for kingfisher.

There are two ways to approach the reserve. You can walk west, through a gate from the car park, and follow the path into the reserve; be warned, though, that this route can get very damp under foot. The other way is to step over the stile by the gate and walk along the top of the bank, watching the river on your left and looking out across the reserve on your right.

Around the car park you can hear blackcap and warblers in spring and early summer. The warblers are a real treat at Waltham. The reed and sedge warblers that chunter away in the long grass and reeds are fairly common in such watery areas, but Waltham is regularly graced with two more, rather special warblers.

The grasshopper warbler is very similar in appearance to the sedge warbler, but you'll rarely see one. Instead, if you visit in the evening in the spring, when the birds pass through in early May, you may hear its remarkable song – a long, mechanical 'reeling' trill, rather like a fishing reel being spun very fast.

The other special warbler to listen out for is the Cetti's warbler. It is similar to a reed warbler, but more stocky, with a reddish-brown back and head. Again, you may not be able to see one, as they skulk in the middle of dense trees or bushes, but their call is an explosive and unmistakeable '*plitt, plitt-plitt, tichut-tichut-tichut chit, chit*' – I always think the irritable little bird is shouting a string of expletives at me for disturbing it.

Spring also brings the cuckoo, insistently calling from the trees and flying over the brooks – I've seen aggressive 'sing-offs' between rivals here, culminating in aerial combat. The watery pools are usually frequented by ducks, including shoveler and teal, and pintail and wigeon in winter, and very occasionally a garganey in spring. The edges are frequented by snipe and the odd greenshank or sandpiper on passage, including green and wood sandpipers, and you'll often hear the squeal of water rail from the reeds.

A peregrine (*see p.36*) or hobby (*see p.26*) can fly over and in the winter short-eared owls (*see p.40*) and hen harriers (*see p.24*) sometimes hunt over the brooks, particularly in the hour or so before dusk. Much more regularly seen are barn owls (*see p.14*), in summer and winter, again usually towards dusk. Encountering these birds is always a special experience and a visit on a spring evening often sends me on my way home with the songs of the warblers still echoing in my ears and with a spring in my step.

Seasonal highlights

◄ *Spring:* garganey, common, green and wood sandpipers
◄ *Spring & summer:* barn owl, grasshopper warbler, Cetti's warbler, blackcap, cuckoo, hobby
◄ *Winter:* Bewick's swan, short-eared owl, hen harrier, barn owl, wigeon, pintail

OTHER SITES IN SUSSEX

Beachy Head

Beachy Head is an extensive area of clifftop grassland, scrub and woods from Birling Gap in the west to Whitbread Hollow in the east, all prime sites for many birds. But the best times for bird-watching here is during the migration periods. Beachy Head sticks out into the English Channel and is the first and last part of Britain that many birds see.

Bird migration is one of the great spectacles of nature and, although wandering around the area watching scrub, branches, grass and every dot that flies overhead can be frustrating, it is never dull. Easterly winds will cause the number of rarities to rise, and it is a good idea to get to the coast at dawn to have the best chance of seeing birds before they fly off during the day.

Birling Gap is usually the first place on my itinerary and you can find it by taking the road that leads through East Dean from the A259, and parking in the National Trust car park. At the bottom of the car park is a set of steps that leads down to the sea. One of the best hot spots, however, is the lane that passes behind the hotel and in front of the group of bungalows. The lane, fences and private gardens shelter migrants, such as redstarts and whinchat, but please do respect the privacy of the home-owners. At the top of the lane is an area of scrub that is a reliable spot for wryneck (see p.52).

From the car park, follow the path that leads to Horseshoe Plantation (which also has a car park), with the road on your left, past some promising bits of scrub that can hide warblers, chats and firecrest. Horseshoe Plantation can teem with warblers, flycatchers and firecrests in the autumn and the rare Pallas's and yellow-browed warblers also favour it. On the other side of the woods, the path skirts an area of scrub where ring ouzel and warblers can be found, along with rarities such as red-backed shrike.

The path curls back towards the cliff and you can walk west, past Belle Tout lighthouse, and inspect the bushes and 'the gully' near the cliff, halfway between Belle Tout and Birling Gap car park. Wheatears, warblers, redstarts and peregrine (see p.36) are all possible.

East of Belle Tout is Shooters Bottom. Park by the road and walk into the small valley known as Chat Vale. The scrub here attracts lots of migrants, such as redstarts, chats and warblers – including migrating Dartford warbler (see p.20) – and ring ouzel. Watch overhead as well for the resident ravens, the distinctive buzzard-sized crows with heavy bills that are now breeding in the area once again.

Beachy Head can get very busy so the birds tend to hide early in the morning, but the middle of the day is a good time to watch for overhead passage of large birds of prey, such as osprey, honey buzzard and marsh harrier.

Whitbread Hollow is further to the east, past the Beachy Head hotel. Thick with dense scrub and bushes, it is another hot spot for warblers, redstarts and ring ouzel. Ring ouzels also gravitate to Francis Bottom in October, and the area of scrub and elder further down the cliffs at Cow Gap is good for wryneck (see p.52). For Francis Bottom and Cow Gap, follow the paths south from Whitbread Hollow towards the series of plateaux that extend towards the sea.

Seasonal highlights
◀ *Spring: pied flycatcher, firecrest, black redstart, occasional hoopoe, osprey*
◀ *Summer: corn bunting, fulmar, stonechat*
◀ *Autumn: pied flycatcher, firecrest, black redstart, redstart, hobby, grasshopper*

warbler, wryneck, nightingale, rare warblers, red-backed shrike, siskin, redpoll, ring ouzel, merlin, short-eared owl, osprey, thrushes, honey buzzard, marsh harrier
◀ *All year: raven, peregrine*

Combe Haven & Filsham Reedbed
Combe Haven and Filsham Reedbed are tucked away off the A259 near Bulverhythe in Hastings. Park near the recreation ground, opposite the Bulverhythe pub, and follow the track alongside the stream, past the caravan park. A secluded valley consisting of the reedbed, managed by the Sussex Wildlife Trust, and water meadows that are often flooded in winter, the area's proximity to the coast makes it an autumnal migration hot spot.

Seasonal highlights
◀ *Spring & summer: hobby, reed warbler*
◀ *Autumn: sand martin, swallow, yellow wagtail, tree pipit*
◀ *Winter: lapwing, snipe, kingfisher, water pipit, occasional bittern*
◀ *All year: bearded tit, Cetti's warbler, water rail*

East Head & West Wittering
East Head is a natural, and ever-changing, sand and shingle spit that juts out into Chichester Harbour, just to the south-east of Thorney Island. Follow the A286 out of Chichester, then take the B2179 to West Wittering, and follow the signs to the West Wittering beach car park. Snowhill Marsh next to the access road attracts golden

plover and black-tailed godwit on passage and in winter little stint and brent geese. Winter may also bring the rare snow bunting that frequent the dunes on the ½-mile (1-km)-long spit.

Seasonal highlights

◀ **Spring:** *osprey, turtle dove, warblers, crests, flycatchers, redstarts, bar-tailed godwit*

◀ **Summer:** *little, common and sandwich terns*

◀ **Autumn:** *warblers, flycatchers, crests and redstarts*

◀ **Winter:** *dunlin, golden, ringed and grey plovers, little stint, black-tailed and bar-tailed godwits, brent geese, red-throated diver, grebes, red-breasted merganser, very rare snow bunting*

◀ **All year:** *Cetti's warbler, grey and red-legged partridges*

Hastings Country Park

Hastings Country Park and the sandstone cliffs on its coastal edge come alive during migration times, particularly early on an autumn morning, from August onwards. There are several main places to visit, from west to east: East Hill; Ecclesbourne Glen; Fairlight Glen; Warren Glen; and Fire Hills. The car parks can be accessed from the A259. The open spaces are good for watching the bird traffic fly south in autumn and the wooded glens and scrub can catch lots of migrating small birds during the spring and autumn seasons.

Seasonal highlights

◀ **Spring:** *firecrest, ring ouzel*

◀ **Summer:** *fulmar*

◀ **Autumn:** *firecrest, ring ouzel, redpoll, crossbill, common and black redstarts, spotted flycatcher, migrating birds of prey*

◀ **All year:** *Dartford warbler, linnet, stonechat, yellowhammer, occasional peregrine falcon*

Seaford Head

Seaford is unusual as a sea-watching site in that it is worth a trip to see the first movements of birds in spring, right through the summer and, of course, for the autumn migration. The cliffs of Seaford Head house around 1,500 kittiwakes through the summer – as well as a few fulmars and the occasional breeding rock pipits. Peregrines (*see p.36*) can also appear at any time. For sea-watching, make your way as far as you can go behind the sea wall at Splash Point.

Seasonal highlights

◀ **Spring:** *skuas, terns, kittiwake, fulmar, little gull, common scoter, divers, black-necked and Slavonian grebes, eider, red-breasted merganser*

◀ **Summer:** *kittiwake, fulmar, shearwaters, storm petrel*

◀ **Autumn:** *skuas, terns, shearwaters, brent geese, red-breasted merganser*

◀ **Winter:** *guillemot, razorbill, divers*

◀ **All year:** *peregrine falcon, rock pipit*

Selsey Bill

Sea-watching is for the committed, the experienced, and those with very good waterproofs. But a whole day's endurance can bag some pretty good birds. And nearby are Selsey West Fields, which will reveal farmland birds most of the year and the possibility of short-eared owl (*see p.40*) and hen harrier (*see p.24*) in winter, and marsh harrier or a rare wader on passage.

Seasonal highlights
- **Spring:** *skuas, terns, little gull, brent geese, common scoter, divers, black-necked and Slavonian grebes, eider, red-breasted merganser, knot, sanderling*
- **Summer:** *shearwaters, storm petrel*
- **Autumn:** *skuas, terns, shearwaters, brent geese, red-breasted merganser, knot, sanderling*
- **Winter:** *guillemot, razorbill, divers*

Warnham Local Nature Reserve

Access to the reserve car park is along the B2237 out of the town. The reserve, along with visitor centre and café, is open 10am-5.30pm or dusk every day. Access to the visitor centre is free, but I recommend taking the longer trail, for which adults pay £1.00. The Mill Pond usually holds a few duck, great crested and little grebes, and a couple of nesting common tern in the summer. A trail leads through the trees and to some boardwalks. The trees here can hold willow and marsh tit, nuthatch and treecreeper, as well as siskin and redpoll in winter. Water rail can be seen around the feeding stations in the woods in winter.

Seasonal highlights
- **Spring:** *very occasional osprey*
- **Summer:** *common tern*
- **Autumn:** *very occasional osprey*
- **Winter:** *water rail, pochard, teal, siskin, redpoll*
- **All year:** *great-crested grebe, little grebe, kingfisher, marsh tit, nuthatch, treecreeper, grey heron, occasional little egret, common buzzard*

Weir Wood Reservoir

Weir Wood is famous as an (almost) annual stopover for osprey, and if you're lucky, they can hang around the western end of the reservoir for a few days or even a week or two. There are usually a few birds to watch out for at any time of year, including kingfisher and mandarin duck, and the feeders by the hide attract tits and nuthatch. Spring and autumn are good times to visit, though, when there's always the chance of a rare wader, such as pectoral sandpiper or night heron.

Seasonal highlights
- **Spring:** *occasional osprey*
- **Summer:** *common tern*
- **Autumn:** *occasional osprey, curlew sandpiper, green sandpiper, little stint*
- **Winter:** *water rail, pochard, siskin, redpoll, snipe*
- **All year:** *great-crested grebe, little grebe, mandarin duck, kingfisher, marsh tit, nuthatch, treecreeper, grey heron, little egret, common buzzard*

RESERVES & OTHER PLACES

AMBERLEY WILD BROOKS
RSPB & Sussex Wildlife Trust
National grid ref. TQ0314
Telephone 01798 875851, 01273 492630
www.rspb.org.uk, www.sussexwt.org.uk

AMBERSHAM COMMON
National grid ref. SU9119
Telephone 01273 476595
(Natural England)
www.naturalengland.org.uk

**ARUNDEL WILDFOWL
& WETLANDS TRUST**
National grid ref. TQ0208
Telephone 01903 883355
www.wwt.org.uk

ASHDOWN FOREST
Ashdown Forest Centre
National grid ref. TQ4332
Telephone 01342 823583
www.ashdownforest.org
Ellison's Pond
National grid ref. TQ4628X
Gills Lap
National grid ref. TQ4632
Millbrook Bottom
National grid ref. TQ4428
Old Lodge Nature Reserve
National grid ref. TQ4630
Old Airstrip
National grid ref. TQ4231
Isle of Thorns
National grid ref. TQ4230

BEACHY HEAD
Birling Gap
National grid ref. TV5596
Horseshoe Plantation
National grid ref. TV5695
Belle Tout
National grid ref. TV5695
Shooters Bottom
National grid ref. TV5795
Beachy Head
National grid ref. TV5895
Cow Gap
National grid ref. TV5995

Whitbread Hollow
National grid ref. TV5996
Telephone 01323 415273
(Eastbourne Borough Council)
www.eastbourne.gov.uk/countryside

**BURTON MILL POND
SUSSEX WILDLIFE TRUST**
National grid ref. TQ9718
Telephone 01273 492630
www.sussexwt.org.uk

CHAILEY COMMON
National grid ref. TQ3820
Telephone 01273 482670
(East Sussex County Council)
www.eastsussex.gov.uk

CHAPEL COMMON
National grid ref. SU8128
Telephone 01730 817322
(South Downs Tourist Information)
www.visitsouthdowns.com

**CHICHESTER CATHEDRAL
& CITY CENTRE**
(open spring & early summer only)
RSPB viewing point
Telephone 01273 775333
www.rspb.org.uk/bnViant

CISSBURY RING
National grid ref. TQ1412
Telephone 01903 221066
(Worthing Tourist Information)

CLIMPING
National grid ref. TQ0000

**COMBE HAVEN &
FILSHAM REEDBED
LOCAL NATURE RESERVE**
National grid ref. TQ7709
Telephone 01273 492630
(Sussex Wildlife Trust)
www.sussexwt.org.uk

**EAST HEAD
NATIONAL TRUST**
National grid ref. SZ7698
Telephone 07799 072593
www.nationaltrust.org.uk

EBERNOE COMMON
SUSSEX WILDLIFE TRUST
National grid ref. SU9727
Telephone 01273 492630
www.sussexwt.org.uk

HASTINGS COUNTRY PARK
East Hill
National grid ref. TQ8309
Ecclesbourne Glen
National grid ref. TQ8310
Fairlight Glen
National grid ref. TQ8510
Fire Hills
National grid ref. TQ8611
Warren Glen
National grid ref. TQ8510
Telephone 01424 451338
(Hastings Borough Council Ranger Service)
www.hastings.gov.uk/hcp

IPING & STEDHAM COMMONS
SUSSEX WILDLIFE TRUST
National grid ref. SU8421 & SU8521
Telephone 01273 492630
www.sussexwt.org.uk

PAGHAM HARBOUR
LOCAL NATURE RESERVE
Visitor Centre
National grid ref. SZ8596
Sidlesham Ferry Pool
National grid ref. SZ855963
Church Norton & Severals
National grid ref. SZ8795
Telephone 01243 641508
www.westsussex.gov.uk/paghamharbour

PETT LEVEL
LOCAL NATURE RESERVE
National grid ref. SU9119
Telephone 01273 476595
(Natural England)
www.naturalengland.org.uk

PEVENSEY LEVELS
Horse Eye Level
National grid ref. TQ6208
Pevensey Bridge Level
National grid ref. TQ6504
Telephone 01273 476595
(Natural England)
www.naturalengland.org.uk

PULBOROUGH BROOKS RSPB
National grid ref. TQ0516
Telephone 01798 875851
www.rspb.org.uk

RYE HARBOUR
NATURE RESERVE
Beach Reserve
National grid ref. TQ9317
Camber Castle
National grid ref. TQ9218
Castle Water
National grid ref. TQ9418
Telephone 01797 227784
www.wildrye.info

SEAFORD HEAD
Splash Point
National grid ref. TV4898

SELSEY
Selsey Bill
National grid ref. SZ8592
Selsey West Fields
National grid ref. SZ8394

SEVEN SISTERS
COUNTRY PARK
Cuckmere Haven
National grid ref. TV5197
Telephone 01323 870280
www.sevensisters.org.uk

THORNEY ISLAND
National grid ref. SU7602

WALTHAM BROOKS
SUSSEX WILDLIFE TRUST
National grid ref. TQ0316
Telephone 01273 492630
www.sussexwt.org.uk

WARNHAM
LOCAL NATURE RESERVE
National grid ref. TQ1732
Telephone 01403 256890
(Horsham District Council
Countryside Services Unit)
www.horshamdistrictcountryside.org

WEIR WOOD
LOCAL NATURE RESERVE
National grid ref. TQ3834
(Friends of Weir Wood)
www.weirwood.me.uk

WOODS MILL
SUSSEX WILDLIFE TRUST
National grid ref. TQ2113
Telephone 01273 492630
www.sussexwt.org.uk

SUSSEX BIRD DIRECTORY

NUMBERS

	Status	Breeding pairs	Winter/Passage
EX	Extinct	—	
VR	Very rare	—	1-10 records in total since 1962
RA	Rare	less than annual	less than annual
VS	Very scarce	1-10 per year	1-20 per year
SC	Scarce	11-100	21-200
FC	Fairly common	101-1000	201-2000
CO	Common	1,001-5,000	2,001-10,000
VC	Very common	5,001-30,000	10,001-60,000
AB	Abundant	30,000+	60,000+

BREEDING STATUS

[R]	Resident, breeds
[BV]	Breeding visitor, but not resident (usually a summer visitor)
[SV]	Summer visitor, but does not breed
[WV]	Winter visitor
[PM]	Passage migrant (spring and autumn)
[V]	Vagrant

DIVERS & GREBES
Red-throated Diver FC
 [WV, PM]
Black-throated Diver SC
 [WV, PM]
Great Northern Diver VS
 [WV, PM]
White-billed Diver VR [V]
Little Grebe SC
 [R, PM, WV]
Great Crested Grebe FC [R,
 PM, WV]
Red-necked Grebe SC
 [WV, PM[
Slavonian Grebe SC
 [WV, PM]

Black-necked Grebe VS
 [WV, PM]

**FULMAR, SHEARWATERS
& PETRELS**
Fulmar FC [BV, PM]
Cory's Shearwater RA [V]
Sooty Shearwater VS [AV]
Manx Shearwater SC [PM]
Mediterranean Shearwater
 RA [V]
Storm Petrel RA [V]
Leach's Petrel RA [V]

**GANNET,
CORMORANT & SHAG**
Gannet FC [PM, SV]

Cormorant SC/CO
 [R/WV]
Shag SC [WV, PM]

**BITTERN, HERONS
& EGRETS**
Bittern VS [WV]
American Bittern VR [V]
Little Bittern RA [V]
Night Heron RA [V]
Squacco Heron VR [V]
Cattle Egret VR [V]
Little Egret FC [PM, WV]
Great White Egret VR [V]
Grey Heron FC [R]
Purple Heron RA [V]

STORKS, IBIS & SPOONBILL

Black Stork VR [V]

White Stork RA [V]

Glossy Ibis VR [V]

Spoonbill VS [PM]

SWANS & GEESE

Mute Swan FC [R]

Bewick's Swan SC [WV]

Whooper Swan VS [WV, PM]

Bean Goose VS [WV, PM]

Pink-footed Goose VS [WV, PM]

White-fronted Goose SC [WV, PM]

Greylag Goose FC [R, WV]

Snow Goose VR [WV]

Canada Goose FC [R, PM]

Barnacle Goose VS [WV]

Brent Goose VC [WV, PM]

Pale-bellied Brent Goose VS [WV]

Black Brant VR [WV]

Red-breasted Goose VR [WV]

Egyptian Goose RA [V]

SHELDUCKS

Ruddy Shelduck VR [V]

Shelduck FC/CO [R, WV]

DUCKS

Mandarin SC [R]

Wigeon CO [WV, PM]

American Wigeon VR [V]

Gadwall VS/FC [R, WV, PM]

Teal SC/CO [R, WV, PM]

Green-winged Teal VR [V]

Mallard CO [R, WV]

Pintail FC [WV, PM, has bred]

Garganey SC/RA [PM, BV, SV]

Blue-winged Teal VR [V]

Shoveler VS/FC [R, WV, PM]

Red-crested Pochard RA [WV, PM, has bred]

Pochard RA/FC [R, WV, PM]

Ring-necked Duck VR [V]

Ferruginous Duck RA [V]

Tufted Duck FC [R, WV]

Scaup SC [WV, PM]

Eider SC [WV, PM]

Long-tailed Duck SC [PM, WV]

Common Scoter CO/FC [PM, WV]

Surf Scoter VR [V]

Velvet Scoter SC [PM, WV]

Goldeneye FC [WV]

Smew VS [WV]

Red-breasted Merganser FC [WV, PM]

Goosander SC [WV, PM]

Ruddy Duck VS/SC [R, WV]

BIRDS OF PREY

Honey Buzzard VS [PM, has bred]

Black Kite RA [V]

Red Kite RA [V]

White-tailed Eagle VR [V]

Marsh Harrier SC/RA [PM, WV]

Hen Harrier SC [WV, PM]

Montagu's Harrier VS [PM, formerly bred]

Goshawk VS [R, WV]

Sparrowhawk FC [R, PM]

Common Buzzard RA/SC [R, PM]

Rough-legged Buzzard RA [WV, PM]

Osprey SC [PM]

Kestrel FC [R, PM]

Red-footed Falcon RA [V]

Merlin SC [WV, PM]

Hobby SC [BV, PM]

Gyr Falcon VR [V]

Peregrine falcon SC [R, PM, WV]

GAMEBIRDS

Black Grouse EX [R]

Red-legged Partridge CO [R]

Grey Partridge FC [R]

Quail SC [BV]

Pheasant VC [R]

Golden Pheasant SC [R]

RAILS, CRAKES, MOORHEN & COOT

Water Rail SC [R, WV, PM]

Spotted Crake VS [PM]

Sora Rail VR [V]

Little Crake VR [V]

Baillon's Crake VR [V]

Corncrake RA [PM, formerly bred]

Moorhen VC [R, WV]

Coot CO [R, WV]

CRANE & BUSTARDS

Crane RA [V]

Little Bustard VR [V]

Great Bustard EX/VR [R, V]

WADERS

Oystercatcher SC/FC [R, PM, WV]

Black-winged Stilt RA [V]

Avocet SC [WV, PM, has bred]

Stone Curlew RA [SV, PM, has bred]

Collared Pratincole VR [V]

Oriental Pratincole VR [V]

Black-winged Pratincole VR [V]

Little Ringed Plover RA/SC [BV, PM]

Ringed Plover FC [R, PM, WV]

Killdeer VR [V]

Kentish Plover VS [PM, formerly bred]

Lesser Sand Plover VR [V]

Greater Sand Plover VR [V]

Dotterel VS [PM]

American Golden Plover
  VR [V]
Golden Plover CO [WV, PM]
Grey Plover CO [WV, PM]
Sociable Plover VR [V]
Lapwing FC/VC [R, WV]
Knot CO/FC [WV, PM]
Sanderling FC [WV, PM]
Semipalmated Sandpiper
  VR [V]
Little Stint SC [PM]
Temminck's Stint VS [PM]
Least Sandpiper VR [V]
White-rumped Sandpiper
  VR [V]
Baird's Sandpiper VR [V]
Pectoral Sandpiper VR [V]
Curlew Sandpiper SC [PM]
Purple Sandpiper SC
  [WV, PM]
Dunlin AB/CO [WV, PM]
Broad-billed Sandpiper
  VR [V]
Stilt Sandpiper VR [V]
Buff-breasted Sandpiper
  VR [V]
Ruff SC [WV, PM]
Jack Snipe SC [WV, PM]
Snipe FC/CO [R, WV]
Great Snipe VR [V]
Long-billed Dowitcher
  VR [V]
Woodcock FC [R, WV]
Black-tailed Godwit CO
  [WV, PM]
Bar-tailed Godwit CO
  [WV, PM]
Whimbrel CO/VS
  [PM, SV, WV]
Curlew CO
  [PM, WV, formerly bred]
Upland Sandpiper VR [V]
Spotted Redshank SC
  [PM, WV]

Redshank FC [R, PM, WV]
Marsh Sandpiper VR [V]
Greenshank FC/SC
  [PM, WV]
Lesser Yellowlegs VR [V]
Green Sandpiper FC/VS
  [PM, WV]
Wood Sandpiper SC [PM]
Terek Sandpiper VR [V]
Common Sandpiper FC/VS
  [PM, WV, has bred]
Spotted Sandpiper VR [V]
Turnstone FC/SC
  [WV, PM, SV]
Wilson's Phalarope VR [V]
Red-necked Phalarope
  RA [PM]
Grey Phalarope VS/RA
  [AV, WV]

SKUAS, GULLS & TERNS
Pomarine Skua SC/VR
  [PM, WV]
Arctic Skua FC/RA
  [PM, WV]
Long-tailed Skua RA [V]
Great Skua SC/VS
  [PM, WV]
Mediterranean Gull SC
  [R, PM, WV, has bred]
Laughing Gull VR [V]
Franklin's Gull VR [V]
Little Gull SC [PM]
Sabine's Gull RA [AV]
Bonaparte's Gull VR [V]
Black-headed Gull CO/AB
  [R, WV, PM]
Slender-billed Gull VR [V]
Ring-billed Gull VR [V]
Common Gull CO
  [WV, PM, has bred]
Lesser Black-backed Gull
  FC/SC [PM, WV, BV]
Herring Gull CO
  [R, PM, WV]

Caspian Gull VR [V]
Yellow-legged Gull SC/VS
  [PM, SV, WV]
Iceland Gull VS [WV, PM]
Glaucous Gull VS
  [WV, PM]
Great Black-backed Gull CO
  [WV, PM]
Kittiwake CO
  [WV, PM, BV]
Ivory Gull VR [V]
Gull-billed Tern RA [V]
Caspian Tern RA [V]
Lesser Crested Tern VR [V]
Sandwich Tern SC/CO
  [BV, PM]
Roseate Tern VS [PM, SV]
Common Tern SC/CO
  [BV, PM]
Arctic Tern FC [PM]
Bridled Tern VR [V]
Sooty Tern VR [V]
Little Tern SC/FC
  [BV, PM]
Whiskered Tern VR [V]
Black Tern FC [PM]
White-winged Black Tern
  RA [V]
Least Tern VR [V]

AUKS
Guillemot FC [WV, PM]
Razorbill FC [WV, PM]
Black Guillemot RA [V]
Little Auk VS [AV, WV]
Puffin VS [PM]

**SANDGROUSE, DOVES
& PIGEONS**
Pallas's Sandgrouse VR [V]
Feral Rock Dove CO [R]
Stock Dove CO [R, WV]
Woodpigeon AB [R, WV]
Collared Dove VC [R]
Turtle Dove CO [SV, PM]

RING-NECKED PARAKEET & CUCKOOS

Ring-necked Parakeet VS [R]

Great Spotted Cuckoo VR [V]

Cuckoo FC [SV]

Yellow-billed Cuckoo VR [V]

OWLS

Barn Owl SC [R]

Dark-breasted Barn Owl VR [V]

Snowy Owl VR [V]

Little Owl FC [R]

Tawny Owl FC [R]

Long-eared Owl RA/VS [R, PM, WV]

Short-eared Owl SC [WV, PM, has bred]

NIGHTJAR & SWIFTS

Nightjar FC [BV]

Swift CO [BV, PM]

Alpine Swift RA [V]

KINGFISHERS, BEE-EATER, ROLLER & HOOPOE

Kingfisher FC [R, WV]

Bee-eater RA [V, has bred]

Roller VR [V]

Hoopoe VS [PM, has bred]

WRYNECK & WOODPECKERS

Wryneck VS [PM, has bred]

Green Woodpecker FC [R]

Great Spotted Woodpecker CO [R]

Lesser Spotted Woodpecker FC [R]

LARKS

White-winged Lark VR [V]

Short-toed Lark VR [V]

Crested Lark VR [V]

Wood Lark VS [R, PM]

Skylark CO [R, PM, WV]

Shore Lark RA [WV]

MARTINS & SWALLOWS

Sand Martin FC/VC [BV, PM]

Crag Martin VR [V]

Cliff Swallow VR [V]

Swallow CO/AB [BV, PM]

Red-rumped Swallow RA [V]

House Martin CO/SC [BV, PM]

PIPITS & WAGTAILS

Richard's Pipit RA [V]

Blyth's Pipit VR [V]

Tawny Pipit VS [V]

Olive-backed Pipit VR [V]

Tree Pipit FC [BV, PM]

Meadow Pipit CO/VC [R, PM]

Red-throated Pipit VR [V]

Rock Pipit VS/FC [R, PM, WV]

Scandinavian Rock Pipit VS [PM]

Water Pipit SC [WV, PM]

Yellow Wagtail FC/CO [BV, PM]

Blue-headed Wagtail VS [V]

Grey-headed Wagtail VR [V]

Ashy-headed Wagtail VR [V]

Grey Wagtail FC [R, PM, WV]

Pied Wagtail CO [R, PM, WV]

White Wagtail VS [PM]

WAXWING, DIPPER, WREN, DUNNOCK & ACCENTOR

Waxwing VS [WV]

Dipper VR [V]

Wren AB [R]

Dunnock AB [R]

Alpine Accentor VR [V]

ROBINS, NIGHTINGALE, BLUETHROAT, CHATS, STARTS & WHEATEARS

Rufous Scrub-Robin VR [V]

Robin AB [R, PM, WV]

Thrush Nightingale VR [V]

Nightingale FC [BV]

Bluethroat VS [PM]

Black Redstart RA/FC/SC [R, PM, WV]

Redstart SC/FC [BV, PM]

Whinchat RA/FC [SV, PM, has bred]

Stonechat SC [R, PM, WV]

Siberian Stonechat VR [V]

Wheatear VS/CO [BV, PM]

Pied Wheatear VR [V]

Black-eared Wheatear VR [V]

Desert Wheatear VR [V]

THRUSHES

Rock Thrush VR [V]

White's Thrush VR [V]

Ring Ouzel SC [PM]

Blackbird AB [R, WV]

Black-throated Thrush VR [V]

Fieldfare CO [PM, WV]

Song Thrush AB/VC [R, PM, WV]

Redwing AB/VC [PM, WV]

Mistle Thrush VC [R, PM, WV]

WARBLERS & CRESTS

Cetti's Warbler VS [R, PM, WV]

Grasshopper Warbler VS/FC [BV, PM]

Savi's Warbler RA [V, probably has bred]

Aquatic Warbler VS [AV]

Sedge Warbler FC/VC [BV, PM]

Paddyfield Warbler VR [V]

Marsh Warbler RA [BV, PM]

Reed Warbler CO/VC
[BV, PM]
Great Reed Warbler RA [V]
Booted Warbler VR [V]
Icterine Warbler RA [V]
Melodious Warbler RA [V]
Dartford Warbler SC
[R, PM, WV]
Subalpine Warbler VR [V]
Sardinian Warbler VR [V]
Barred Warbler VS [AV]
Lesser Whitethroat CO
[BV, PM]
Whitethroat VC [BV, PM]
Garden Warbler VC [BV, PM]
Blackcap VC/SC
[BV, PM, WV]
Greenish Warbler VR [V]
Pallas's Leaf Warbler VS[AV]
Yellow-browed Warbler
VS [V]
Hume's Leaf Warbler VR [V]
Radde's Warbler VR [V]
Dusky Warbler VR [V]
Western Bonelli's Warbler
VR [V]
Wood Warbler VS [SV, PM]
Chiffchaff VC/SC
[BV, PM, WV]
Willow Warbler AB [BV, PM]
Goldcrest VC/CO
[R, PM, WV]
Firecrest RA/SC
[BV, PM, WV]

FLYCATCHERS
Spotted Flycatcher FC
[BV, PM]
Red-breasted Flycatcher
RA [AV]
Pied Flycatcher SC
[PM, has bred]

TITS
Bearded Tit VS/SC
[R, PM, WV]

Long-tailed Tit VC [R]
Marsh Tit CO [R]
Willow Tit FC [R]
Crested Tit VR [V]
Coal Tit VC [R]
Continental Coal Tit RA [V]
Blue Tit AB [R]
Great Tit AB [R]

**NUTHATCHES,
CREEPERS, PENDULINE
TIT & GOLDEN ORIOLE**
Nuthatch VC [R]
Wallcreeper VR [V]
Treecreeper VC [R]
Penduline Tit RA [AV]
Golden Oriole VS
[PM, SV, may have bred]

SHRIKES
Isabelline Shrike VR [V]
Red-backed Shrike VS [PM,
formerly bred]
Lesser Grey Shrike VR [V]
Great Grey Shrike VS
[WV, PM]
Woodchat Shrike RA [V]

CROWS
Jay VC [R, PM, WV]
Magpie VC [R]
Nutcracker VR [V]
Chough EX/VR [R, V]
Jackdaw VC [R]
Rook VC [R]
Carrion Crow VC [R]
Hooded Crow VS [V]
Raven VR [R, V]

STARLINGS
Starling AB [R, PM, WV]
Rose-coloured Starling
VR [V]

SPARROWS & FINCHES
House Sparrow AB [R]
Tree Sparrow SC
[R, PM, WV]

Chaffinch AB [R, PM, WV]
Brambling FC [WV, PM]
Serin VS [PM, has bred]
Greenfinch VC [R, PM, WV]
Goldfinch CO [R, PM, WV]
Siskin VS/CO [BV, WV, PM]
Linnet VC [R, PM, WV]
Twite SC [WV, PM]
Redpoll FC [BV, PM, WV]
Northern Redpoll VR [WV]
Crossbill SC
[WV, periodically breeds]
Parrot Crossbill VR [V]
Trumpeter Finch VR [V]
Scarlet Rosefinch RA [V]
Bullfinch VC [R]
Hawfinch SC/VS [R, PM]

**NORTH AMERICAN
PASSERINES**
Black & White Warbler
VR [V]
Blackpoll Warbler VR [V]
White-throated Sparrow
VR [V]
Slate-coloured Junco VR [V]
Northern Oriole VR [V]

BUNTINGS
Lapland Bunting VS
[PM, WV]
Snow Bunting SC [PM, WV]
Yellowhammer VC [R]
Cirl Bunting EX/VR [R, V]
Rock Bunting VR [V]
Ortolan Bunting VS [AV]
Rustic Bunting VR [V]
Little Bunting VR [V]
Reed Bunting CO
[R, PM, WV]
Pallas's Reed Bunting
VR [V]
Black-headed Bunting
VR [V]
Corn Bunting FC [R]

INDEX